SpringerBriefs in Economics

For further volumes:
http://www.springer.com/series/8876

Gagari Chakrabarti · Chitrakalpa Sen

Momentum Trading on the Indian Stock Market

Springer

Gagari Chakrabarti
Presidency University
Kolkata, West Bengal
India

Chitrakalpa Sen
Auro University
Surat, Gujarat
India

ISSN 2191-5504
ISBN 978-81-322-1126-6
DOI 10.1007/978-81-322-1127-3
Springer New Delhi Heidelberg New York Dordrecht London

ISSN 2191-5512 (electronic)
ISBN 978-81-322-1127-3 (eBook)

Library of Congress Control Number: 2013933591

© The Author(s) 2013

This work is subject to copyright. All rights are reserved by the Publisher, whether the whole or part of the material is concerned, specifically the rights of translation, reprinting, reuse of illustrations, recitation, broadcasting, reproduction on microfilms or in any other physical way, and transmission or information storage and retrieval, electronic adaptation, computer software, or by similar or dissimilar methodology now known or hereafter developed. Exempted from this legal reservation are brief excerpts in connection with reviews or scholarly analysis or material supplied specifically for the purpose of being entered and executed on a computer system, for exclusive use by the purchaser of the work. Duplication of this publication or parts thereof is permitted only under the provisions of the Copyright Law of the Publisher's location, in its current version, and permission for use must always be obtained from Springer. Permissions for use may be obtained through RightsLink at the Copyright Clearance Center. Violations are liable to prosecution under the respective Copyright Law. The use of general descriptive names, registered names, trademarks, service marks, etc. in this publication does not imply, even in the absence of a specific statement, that such names are exempt from the relevant protective laws and regulations and therefore free for general use.

While the advice and information in this book are believed to be true and accurate at the date of publication, neither the authors nor the editors nor the publisher can accept any legal responsibility for any errors or omissions that may be made. The publisher makes no warranty, express or implied, with respect to the material contained herein.

Printed on acid-free paper

Springer is part of Springer Science+Business Media (www.springer.com)

Contents

1 Introduction 1
   References 4

**2 Trends in Indian Stock Market: Scope for Designing
Profitable Trading Rule?** 5
  2.1   Introduction 5
  2.2   Trends and Latent Structure in Indian Stock Market 6
       2.2.1   The Market and the Sectors: Bombay
              Stock Exchange 6
       2.2.2   The Market and the Sectors: National
              Stock Exchange 7
  2.3   Detection of Structural Break in Volatility 8
       2.3.1   Detection of Multiple Structural Breaks
              in Variance: The ICSS Test 9
  2.4   Identifying Trends in Indian Stock Market:
       The Methodology 12
  2.5   Trends and Latent Structure in Indian Stock Market:
       Bombay Stock Exchange 14
  2.6   Trends and Latent Structure in Indian Stock Market:
       National Stock Exchange 33
  References 51

3 Possible Investment Strategies in Indian Stock Market 55
  3.1   Introduction 55
  3.2   Investment Strategies in BSE 56
       3.2.1   Portfolio Construction in BSE: 2005–2012 57
       3.2.2   Portfolio Construction in BSE in the Pre-crisis Period:
              2005–2008 59
       3.2.3   Portfolio Construction in BSE in the Post-crisis Period:
              2008–2012 61

3.3	Investment Strategies in NSE		63
	3.3.1 Portfolio Construction in NSE: 2005–2012		63
	3.3.2 Portfolio Construction in NSE: 2005–2008		65
	3.3.3 Portfolio Construction in NSE: 2008–2012		66
Reference			68

4 Investigation into Optimal Trading Rules in Indian Stock Market 69

4.1	Introduction	69
4.2	Literature Review	70
4.3	Objectives of the Chapter	71
4.4	Dataset	71
4.5	Finding the Optimum Trading Rule	72
4.6	How the Trading Rule Varies Depending on the Performance of the Economy	72
4.7	Finding the Optimum Trading Rule for BSE Indexes	73
	4.7.1 Visual Analysis of Autocorrelation	73
	4.7.2 Trading Rule in BSE	78
4.8	Finding the Optimum Trading Rule for the NSE Indexes	89
	4.8.1 Visual Analysis of Autocorrelation	90
	4.8.2 Trading Rule in NSE	94
4.9	Behavior of Indexes Before and After the Crisis	102
	4.9.1 Behavior of NSE Indexes Before and After the Crisis	102
	4.9.2 Behavior of BSE Indexes Before and After the Crisis	105
4.10	The Optimal Trading Rule in India: The Epilogue	108
References		110

Figures

Fig. 2.1	Movements in factor scores, BSE (2005–2012)	16
Fig. 2.2	Cycle in the BSE return (2005–2012)	17
Fig. 2.3	BSE conditional variance (2005–2012)	18
Fig. 2.4	Cycle in the factor score BSE conditional variance (2005–2012)	19
Fig. 2.5	Return-risk relationship BSE (2005–2012)	21
Fig. 2.6	Movements in factor scores, BSE (2005–2008)	23
Fig. 2.7	Cycle in the BSE return (2005–2008)	24
Fig. 2.8	Cycle in the factor score BSE conditional variance (2005–2008)	25
Fig. 2.9	Return-risk relationship BSE (2005–2008)	26
Fig. 2.10	Movements in factor scores, BSE (2008–2012)	28
Fig. 2.11	Cycle in the BSE (2008–2012)	29
Fig. 2.12	Cycle in the factor score BSE conditional variance (2008–2012)	30
Fig. 2.13	Return-risk relationship BSE (2008–2012)	31
Fig. 2.14	Nature of eigenvalue for BSE (2005–2012)	32
Fig. 2.15	Movements in factor scores for factor 1 (NSE sector) (2005–2012)	35
Fig. 2.16	Movements in factor scores for factor 2 (NSE market) (2005–2012)	36
Fig. 2.17	Cycle in the sectoral return (NSE) (2005–2012)	36
Fig. 2.18	Cycle in the market return (NSE) (2005–2012)	36
Fig. 2.19	NSE sectoral conditional variance (2005–2012)	37
Fig. 2.20	Cycle in the NSE sectoral conditional variance (2005–2012)	38
Fig. 2.21	Cycle of risk-return relationship at NSE sectoral level (2005–2012)	38
Fig. 2.22	NSE market conditional variance (2005–2012)	39
Fig. 2.23	Cycle in the NSE market conditional variance (2005–2012)	39
Fig. 2.24	Cycle of risk-return relationship at NSE Market level (2005–2012)	39

Fig. 2.25	Movements in factor scores, NSE (2005–2008)	42
Fig. 2.26	Cycles in the NSE return (2005–2008)	42
Fig. 2.27	Cycle in the factor score conditional variance (NSE: 2005–2008)	43
Fig. 2.28	Return-risk relationship NSE (2005–2008)	44
Fig. 2.29	Movements in factor scores, NSE (2008–2012)	47
Fig. 2.30	Cycles in the sectoral and market return (NSE) (2008–2012)	47
Fig. 2.31	Cycle in the NSE conditional variance (2008–2012)	49
Fig. 2.32	Return-risk relationship BSE (2008–2012)	50
Fig. 2.33	Nature of eigenvalue for first factor in NSE (2005–2012)	50

Tables

Table 2.1	Correlation matrix among BSE index returns (2005–2012)	15
Table 2.2	Factor loadings in the single factor extracted: entire period	16
Table 2.3	Application of EGARCH model on factor score for BSE (2005–2012)	18
Table 2.4	Correlation matrix among BSE index returns (2005–2008)	22
Table 2.5	Factor loadings in the single factor extracted: pre-crisis period	23
Table 2.6	Application of EGARCH model on factor score for BSE (2005–2008)	25
Table 2.7	Correlation matrix among BSE index returns (2008–2012)	27
Table 2.8	Factor loadings in the single factor extracted: post-crisis period	28
Table 2.9	Application of EGARCH model on factor score for BSE (2008–2012)	30
Table 2.10	Correlation matrix among NSE index returns (2005–2012)	34
Table 2.11	Factor loadings in the factors extracted: entire period	35
Table 2.12	Correlation matrix among NSE index returns (2005–2008)	40
Table 2.13	Factor loadings in the factors extracted: pre-crisis period (NSE)	41
Table 2.14	Correlation matrix among NSE index returns (2008–2012)	45
Table 2.15	Factor loadings in the factors extracted (NSE): post-crisis period	46
Table 2.16	Application of EGARCH model on first factor score for NSE (2008–2012)	48
Table 2.17	Application of EGARCH model on second factor score for NSE (2008–2012)	49

Table 3.1	Categorization of BSE indexes: 2005–2012	57
Table 3.2	Portfolio construction in BSE in the pre-crisis period: 2005–2008	60
Table 3.3	Portfolio construction in BSE in the post-crisis period: 2008–2012	61
Table 3.4	Portfolio construction in NSE (2005–2012)	64
Table 3.5	Portfolio construction in NSE: 2005–2008	65
Table 3.6	Portfolio construction in NSE: 2008–2012	67
Table 4.1	Regression result of AUTO on a constant (general buy and sell strategy)	79
Table 4.2	Regression of AUTO based on the trading rule	80
Table 4.3	Regression result of BANK on a constant (general buy and sell strategy)	80
Table 4.4	Regression of BANK based on the trading rule	80
Table 4.5	Regression result of CD on a constant (general buy and sell strategy)	81
Table 4.6	Regression of CD based on the trading rule	81
Table 4.7	Regression result of FMCG on a constant (general buy and sell strategy)	82
Table 4.8	Regression of FMCG based on the trading rule	82
Table 4.9	Regression result of HC on a constant (general buy and sell strategy)	82
Table 4.10	Regression of HC based on the trading rule	83
Table 4.11	Regression result of IT on a constant (general buy and sell strategy)	83
Table 4.12	Regression of IT based on the trading rule	84
Table 4.13	Regression result of METAL on a constant (general buy and sell strategy)	84
Table 4.14	Regression of METAL based on the trading rule	84
Table 4.15	Regression result of ONG on a constant (general buy and sell strategy)	85
Table 4.16	Regression of ONG based on the trading rule	85
Table 4.17	Regression result of POWER on a constant (general buy and sell strategy)	85
Table 4.18	Regression of POWER based on the trading rule	86
Table 4.19	Regression result of PSU on a constant (general buy and sell strategy)	86
Table 4.20	Regression of PSU based on the trading rule	87
Table 4.21	Regression result of SENSEX on a constant (general buy and sell strategy)	87
Table 4.22	Regression of SENSEX based on the trading rule	87
Table 4.23	Regression result of TECK on a constant (general buy and sell strategy)	88
Table 4.24	Regression of TECK based on the trading rule	88

Table 4.25	Regression result of CG on a constant (general buy and sell strategy)	89
Table 4.26	Regression of CG based on the trading rule	89
Table 4.27	Regression result of NSE consumption on a constant (general buy and sell strategy)	94
Table 4.28	Regression of NSE consumption based on the trading rule	94
Table 4.29	Regression result of NSE energy on a constant (general buy and sell strategy)	95
Table 4.30	Regression of NSE Energy based on the trading rule	95
Table 4.31	Regression result of NSE finance on a constant (general buy and sell strategy)	95
Table 4.32	Regression of NSE finance based on the trading rule	96
Table 4.33	Regression result of NSE FMCG on a constant (general buy and sell strategy)	96
Table 4.34	Regression of NSE FMCG based on the trading rule	96
Table 4.35	Regression result of NSE INFRA on a constant (general buy and sell strategy)	97
Table 4.36	Regression of NSE INFRA based on the trading rule	97
Table 4.37	Regression result of NSE IT on a constant (general buy and sell strategy)	97
Table 4.38	Regression of NSE IT based on the trading rule	97
Table 4.39	Regression result of NSE METAL on a constant (general buy and sell strategy)	98
Table 4.40	Regression of NSE METAL based on the trading rule	98
Table 4.41	Regression result of NSE MNC on a constant (general buy and sell strategy)	99
Table 4.42	Regression of NSE MNC based on the trading rule	99
Table 4.43	Regression result of NSE PHARMA on a constant (general buy and sell strategy)	99
Table 4.44	Regression of NSE PHARMA based on the trading rule	99
Table 4.45	Regression result of NSE PSE on a constant (general buy and sell strategy)	100
Table 4.46	Regression of NSE PSE based on the trading rule	100
Table 4.47	Regression result of NSE PSU on a constant (general buy and sell strategy)	101
Table 4.48	Regression of NSE PSU based on the trading rule	101
Table 4.49	Regression result of NSE SERVICE on a constant (general buy and sell strategy)	101
Table 4.50	Regression of NSE SERVICE based on the trading rule	101
Table 4.51	General buy and sell strategy in NSE in pre-crisis period	102
Table 4.52	Trading rule in NSE in pre-crisis period	103
Table 4.53	General buy and sell strategy in NSE in post-crisis period	103

Table 4.54	Trading rule in NSE in post-crisis period	104
Table 4.55	General buy and sell strategy in BSE in pre-crisis period	105
Table 4.56	Trading rule in BSE in pre-crisis period	106
Table 4.57	General buy and sell strategy in BSE in post-crisis period	107
Table 4.58	Trading Rule in BSE in Post-Crisis Period	107

Graphs

Graph 4.1	ACF for BSE AUTO	74
Graph 4.2	ACF for BSE BANK	74
Graph 4.3	ACF for BSE CD	74
Graph 4.4	ACF for BSE FMCG	75
Graph 4.5	ACF for BSE HC	75
Graph 4.6	ACF for BSE IT	75
Graph 4.7	ACF for BSE METAL	76
Graph 4.8	ACF for BSE ONG	76
Graph 4.9	ACF for BSE POWER	76
Graph 4.10	ACF for BSE PSU	77
Graph 4.11	ACF for BSE SENSEX	77
Graph 4.12	ACF for BSE TECK	77
Graph 4.13	ACF for BSE CG	78
Graph 4.14	ACF for CONSUMPTION	90
Graph 4.15	ACF for ENERGY	90
Graph 4.16	ACF for FINANCE	91
Graph 4.17	ACF for FMCG	91
Graph 4.18	ACF for INFRA	91
Graph 4.19	ACF for IT	92
Graph 4.20	ACF for METAL	92
Graph 4.21	ACF for MNC	92
Graph 4.22	ACF for PHARMA	93
Graph 4.23	ACF for PSE	93
Graph 4.24	ACF for PSU	93
Graph 4.25	ACF for SERVICE	94

About the Authors

Dr. Gagari Chakrabarti completed her Master's, M.Phil and Doctorate in Economics at the University of Calcutta and is currently working as an Assistant Professor at the prestigious Presidency University in Kolkata, India. Her area of specialization is Financial Economics and the application of econometrics in financial economics. She has several national and international publications to her credit.

Chitrakalpa Sen is an Assistant Professor in Economics at Auro University, Surat. He completed his Master's in Economics at Calcutta University and his Ph.D. at the West Bengal University of Technology. Dr. Sen's area of interest is financial economics, econometrics, and the nonlinear application of econometrics in financial time series. He has presented his works at several national and international conferences and in journals.

Chapter 1
Introduction

A market is the combined behaviour of thousands of people responding to information, misinformation and whim.

Kenneth Chang

Resolving issues like "how and why markets work? ... and work well?"[1] are often concerns of the so-called mainstream economists. The query dates back to Adam Smith who conjectured a self-regulating economic system that heads towards a stable equilibrium, as individual economic agents pursue their divergent, often conflicting self-interest. No vulnerabilities on the part of the market were feared, the markets were supposed to be "fundamentally stable". The illusion continued to impinge on ideas of other noted economists of the day such as Ricardo, Say, Marshal, and Walrus. Out of this evolved a related chimera: in a fundamentally stable market, asset prices truly reflect fundamentals and are fairly priced. The optimistic belief was too strong to be uprooted even by the great depression of the 1930s. The post-war economic theory saw a resurgence of the idea of rationality and efficiency of the market: "they breathed new life into the old fallacy".[2]

One of the most celebrated post-war economics theories is the efficient market hypothesis (Fama 1970). The theory propagated the 'fact' that it may be possible to beat some of the markets all the time and all the markets some of the times but it would be impossible to beat all the markets all the time. The efficient market hypothesis tells that it would be impossible to make consistent profit from any asset market. The market is able to process new information instantaneously and this is reflected properly in the asset price. In a stock market, where numerous profit motivated investors are playing with similar objectives, where each of them prefers a stock with high return than a stock with low return and a stock with low risk to a stock with high risk, with no insider knowledge available to anyone (at least legally), each investor can expect to earn only a fair return for the risks undertaken (Hagin 1979). According to Cootner (1964), "If any substantial group of buyers thought prices were too low, their buying would force up the prices. The reverse would be true for sellers. Except for appreciation due to earnings retention, the conditional expectation of tomorrow's price, given today's price, is today's price. In such a world, the only price changes that would occur are those that result

---

[1] Crisis Economics, Nouriel Roubini and Stephen Mihm 2010, Allen Lane, p. 39.
[2] Crisis Economics, Nouriel Roubini and Stephen Mihm 2010, Allen Lane, p. 41.

G. Chakrabarti and C. Sen, *Momentum Trading on the Indian Stock Market,*
SpringerBriefs in Economics, DOI: 10.1007/978-81-322-1127-3_1,
© The Author(s) 2013

from new information. Since there is no reason to expect that information to be non-random in appearance, the period-to-period price changes of a stock should be random movements, statistically independent of one another".

The efficient market hypothesis has been challenged time and again on various grounds. One of the most potent of these is on the basis of consistently profitable trading strategies. According to the efficient market hypothesis, the performance of portfolios of stocks should be independent of past returns (Hon and Tonks 2003). However, empirical studies have shown that stock prices are not actually independent of past returns. They exhibit positive autocorrelation for a very long time which decays slowly. Momentum trading is one of the trading strategies which bank on this autocorrelation and buy and sell accordingly to make consistent profits. Since its discovery by DeBondt and Thaler (1985), the benefits of momentum strategies have been documented in many markets. Momentum trading, in simple words, means buying stocks which exhibit past overperformance.[3] Momentum trading is built on the rule that stocks which have been performing well, more precisely, better than the market for a predefined historical period, will tend to perform strongly in the coming periods as well. It has been shown that these momentum stocks outperform the market significantly in future periods as well. As Vanstone (2010) puts aptly, with momentum trading strategies, the investors hitch a ride on the stronger stocks. The efficient market hypothesis, is however unable to explain this phenomenon. Fama himself referred this as "the premier unexplained anomaly". The proponents of efficient market theory continue to call momentum trading a result of irrational investor behavior or "psychological biases" (Abreu and Brunnermeier 2003). The study of momentum in a particular asset market is of utmost importance, as in extreme cases, it may cause herding, bubble, and subsequent crash[4] (Vayanos and Wooley 2009). A possible reason for existence of momentum in the stock market is that the market is at most semi-strong efficient and exhibits a certain degree of long-term memory, i.e., once a shock is propagated into the system, it does not die down instantly as proposed by the efficient market theory, but decays slowly. Thus, the presence of momentum trading and the resultant denial of efficient market hypothesis have implications for financial market theories as well as for government policies. And, the area has emerged as the financial market analysts' delight.

This study is an exploration of the Indian stock market for the possible presence of momentum trading. One thing, however, is to be noted. While it is true that momentum trading, generating speculative bubble may bring in its train a financial market crash, its nature on the other hand might depend on the nature of the economy itself. The study, while exploring the presence and nature of momentum trading in the Indian stock market in recent years tries to relate it to the significant structural breaks in the Indian or global economy. To be precise, it tries to relate the instability in the stock market possibly to the speculative trading in the market:

---

[3] http://www.incrediblecharts.com/technical/momentum_trading.php

[4] http://www.voxeu.org/article/capital-market-theory-after-efficient-market-hypothesis

1 Introduction

whether it is human psychology that drives financial markets. In that process, the choice of a significant structural break has been obvious: the global financial meltdown of 2007–2008—a crisis that has often been referred to as the worst financial crisis ever since the one related to the great depression of 1929.

While analyzing the nature of momentum trading in the Indian stock market around the financial crisis of 2007–2008, the study takes into account two major representatives of the market, Bombay stock index (BSE) and National stock index (NSE), over the period 2005–2012. This study seeks to answer a few important questions. First of all, it tries to unveil the underlying structure of the market. In that process, it examines the following issues:

- What has been the latent structure in the Indian stock market around the crisis of 2007–2008? Does the structure hint scope for designing a profitable trading strategy?
- Is it possible to construct a profitable portfolio in the Indian stock market?
- Is there any profitable trading strategy in the Indian stock market?

While exploring these issues, the study delves deeper and breaks the whole period into two sub-periods, before the crisis of 2008 and after the crisis of 2008. The rationale beneath this segregation is to see whether there has been any discernible change in the market structure before and after the shock.

There have been some studies that have explored some of these issues albeit in an isolated manner. An empirical analysis in the Indian context addressing all such issues, particularly in the context of recent financial meltdowns, is however, lacking in the field. The present study is a comprehensive, analytical study (instead of being theoretical only) on momentum trading, thus trying to fill the void in the literature.

After this introductory chapter, the trajectory of the study will be as follows:

Chapter 2 explores the latent structure in the Indian stock market, along with its sectors, around the financial crisis. To understand the market structure, the study makes use of exploratory factor analysis. It also tracks the factor scores along with the cycles in the respective indexes to scrutinize the underlying market behavior. Specifically, the chapter seeks to address the following issues:

- How the market has behaved over the period of study? Has there been any latent structure in the market?
- What are the trends at sectoral level? Are they similar, or otherwise, to the market trends?
- Are the trends independent of the selection of the stock market exchanges?
- Whether and how financial crisis could affect the market trends? The rationale beneath such analyses is to see whether there has been any discernible change in the market structure before and after the shock. A clear behavioral pattern would hint towards an inefficient market and possible scope for designing profitable portfolio mix.

Chapter 3 tries to find an optimal portfolio mix in the Indian stock market. It considers different parameters like risk, return, risk-adjusted return, and market risk to construct portfolios at market and sectoral levels. It then considers whether the choice of the portfolio is independent of the selection of the stock market exchanges and can avoid the cycles of the economy.

Chapter 4 deals with momentum trading and possibility of a profitable trading strategy in the Indian stock market. It does so by examining the historical moving averages of the indexes. According to the trading rule an investor should buy when price is above some moving average of historical prices and sell when price falls below some moving average. The study will consider several moving averages, short run, medium run, and long run, and will see whether the general buy and sell strategies fare better than the holding strategy based on the moving average. Existence of a momentum strategy would reaffirm the doubt that the Indian stock market is not efficient. It will put a question mark to the invincibility of the market, as suggested by the efficient market hypothesis.

The study concludes by pointing towards the implications of the findings at investment and policy level.

References

Abreu D, Brunnermeier MK (2003) Bubbles and crashes. Econometrica 71(1):173–204

Cootner P (ed) (1964) The random character of stock market prices. M.I.T, Cambridge

DeBondt WFM, Thaler RH (1985) Does the stock market overreact? J Financ 40:793–805

Fama E (1970) Efficient capital markets: a review of theory and empirical work. J Finan 25(2):383–417

Hagin R (1979) Modern portfolio theory. Dow Jones-Irwin, Homewood, 11–13 and 89–91

Hon MT, Tonks I (2003) Momentum in the UK stock market. J Multinational Financ Manage 13(1):43–70

Vanstone B (2010) Momentum. http://epublications.bond.edu.au/infotech_pubs. Accessed 12 Nov 2012

Vayanos D, Woolley P (2009) Capital market theory after the efficient market hypothesis. http://www.voxeu.org/article/capital-market-theory-after-efficient-market-hypothesis. Accessed 19 Nov 2012

Chapter 2
Trends in Indian Stock Market: Scope for Designing Profitable Trading Rule?

Abstract This chapter explores the latent structure in the Indian stock market, along with its sectors, around the financial crisis. To understand the market structure, the study makes use of exploratory factor analysis. It also tracks the factor scores along with the cycles in the respective indexes to scrutinize the underlying market behavior. Apart from looking for the latent structure, the chapter seeks to explore the following issues: How the market has behaved over the period of study? What are the trends at sectoral level? Are they similar, or otherwise to the market trends? Are the trends independent of the selection of the stock market exchanges and whether, and how financial crisis could affect such trends? The rationale behind such analyses is to see whether there has been any discernible change in the market structure before and after the shock. A clear behavioral pattern would hint toward an inefficient market and possible scope for designing profitable portfolio mix.

Keywords Indian stock market · Bombay stock exchange · National stock exchange · Stock market cycle · Structural break · Exploratory factor analysis

> *In the business world, the rearview mirror is always clearer than the windshield.*
> Warren Buffett

2.1 Introduction

The presence of momentum trading and the resultant trial put on the efficient market hypothesis have attracted the attention of financial analysts and researchers. Momentum trading is a result of irrational investor behavior or "psychological biases" or "biased self-attribution", and may lead to, in extreme cases, herd behavior, formation of bubble, and subsequent panic and crashes in financial market. The speculative bubble generated by momentum trading inflate, becomes

G. Chakrabarti and C. Sen, *Momentum Trading on the Indian Stock Market*,
SpringerBriefs in Economics, DOI: 10.1007/978-81-322-1127-3_2,
© The Author(s) 2013

'self-fulfilling' until they eventually burst with their far-reaching, ruinous impact on real economy. The crash is usually followed by an irrational, negative bubble. Momentum trading thus leads to irrational movement in prices in both directions and its presence is a serious attack on the myth that a capitalist system is self-regulating heading toward a stable equilibrium. Rather, as noted by Shiller and others, it is an unstable system susceptible to "irrational exuberance" and "irrational pessimism".

Ours is a study that explores the possible presence of momentum trading in the Indian stock market in recent years, particularly in light of the recent global financial melt-down of 2007–2008. Given the close connection between financial melt-down and speculative trading, the relevance of the study is obvious. The study starts with an exploration of the trend and latent structure in the Indian stock market around the crisis and eventually tries to relate the instability to the speculative trading.

2.2 Trends and Latent Structure in Indian Stock Market

While analyzing the trends in the Indian stock market around the financial crisis of 2007–2008, the study uses some benchmark stock market indexes along with different sectoral indexes. The Bombay stock exchange (BSE) and the National stock exchange (NSE) are the two oldest and largest stock market exchanges in India and hence, could be taken as representatives of the Indian stock market. The study analyzes the trends, their similarities and dissimilarities, in the two exchanges to get a complete description of Indian stock market movements. While analyzing the market trends the study concentrates on the following:

How the market has behaved over the period of study. Has there been any latent structure in the market?
What are the trends at sectoral level? Are they similar, or otherwise, to the market trends?
Are the trends independent of the selection of the stock market exchanges?
Whether and how financial crisis could affect the market trends?

Before we go into the detailed analysis let us briefly report on the market index and the sectoral indexes that the study picks up from the two exchanges. The study uses daily price data for all the market and sectoral indexes for the period ranging from January 2005 to September 2012. The price data are then used to calculate daily return series using the formula $R_t = \ln(P_t/P_{t-1})$, where P_t is the price on the t'th day.

2.2.1 The Market and the Sectors: Bombay Stock Exchange

The study considers BSE SENSEX or BSE Sensitive Index or BSE 30 as the market index from BSE. BSE SENSEX, which started in January 1986 is a value-weighted index composed of 30 largest and most actively traded stocks in BSE. The SENSEX is regarded as the pulse of the domestic stock markets in India. These companies account for around 50 % of the market capitalization of the BSE. The base value of the SENSEX is 100 on April 1, 1979, and the base year of BSE-SENSEX is 1978–1979. Initially, the index was calculated on the 'full market capitalization' method. However, it has switched to the free float method since September 2003. The stocks represent different sectors such as, housing related, capital goods, telecom, diversified, finance, transport equipment, metal, metal products and mining, FMCG, information technology, power, oil and gas, and healthcare.

As far as the sectoral indexes are concerned, we select 11 market capitalization weighted sectoral indexes introduced by BSE in 1999. These are BSE AUTO, BSE BANKEX, BSE CD, BSE CG, BSE FMCG, BSE IT, BSE HC, BSE PSU, BSE METAL, BSE ONG, and BSE POWER. Of these indexes, only BANKEX has its base year in 2000. All the others have base year in 1999 with base value of 100 in February 1999. The indexes represent different sectors in the Indian economy namely, automobile, banking, consumer durables, capital goods, fast moving consumer goods, information technology, healthcare, public sector unit, metal, oil and gas, and power, respectively.

2.2.2 The Market and the Sectors: National Stock Exchange

The NSE is the stock exchange located at Mumbai, India. In terms of market capitalization, it is the 11th largest index in the world. By daily turnover and number of trades, for both equities and derivative trading it is the largest index in India. NSE has a market capitalization of around US$1 trillion and over 1,652 listings as of July 2012. NSE is mutually owned by a set of leading financial institutions, banks, insurance companies, and other financial intermediaries in India but its ownership and management operate as separate entities. In 2011, NSE was the third largest stock exchange in the world in terms of the number of contracts traded in equity derivatives. It is the second fastest growing stock exchange in the world with a recorded growth of 16.6 %. As far as the sectoral indexes are concerned, we select some market capitalization weighted sectoral indexes introduced by NSE. These are CNX BANK, CNX COMMO, CNX ENERGY, CNX FINANCE, CNX FMCG, CNX IT, CNX METALS, CNX MNC, CNX PHARMA, CNX PSU BANK, CNX PSE, CNX INFRA, and CNX SERVICES. The indexes represent different sectors in the Indian economy namely Bank, Consumptions sector, Energy, Finance, FMCG, IT, Metal, MNC, Pharmaceutical, Public Sector Unit, Infrastructure, and Services.

The study is conducted and market trends are analyzed over three phases in the Indian stock market:

1. The entire period: 2005 January to 2012 September. The trends obtained for this entire period could be taken as the 'average' market trend.
2. The prologue of crisis: 2005 January to 2008 January.
3. The aftermath of crisis: 2008 February to 2012 September.

The phases are constructed using the methods of detecting a structural break in a financial time series. Any financial crisis could well be thought of as a switch in regime that is often reflected in a structural break in the market volatility. In that way, a financial crisis could possibly be associated with a volatility break or regime switches that might lead to financial crises. While identifying volatility breaks, we use the same methodology, introduced originally by Inclan and Tiao (1994), and used in our earlier studies (2011, 2012). We recapitulate the methodology briefly in the following sections.

2.3 Detection of Structural Break in Volatility

The parameters of a typical time series do not remain constant over time. It makes paradigm shifts in regular intervals. The time of this shift is the structural break and the period between two breakpoints is known as a regime. There have been several studies aimed at measuring the breakpoints. As usual, a majority of them are in the stock market. As only the algorithm used to detect the breakpoints is important rather than the underlying time series, the following section discusses those studies with important breakthroughs in the algorithm.

The first group of studies was able to detect only one unknown structural breakpoint. Perron (1990, 1997a), Hansen (1990, 1992), Banerjee et al. (1992), Perron and Vogelsang (1992), Chu and White (1992), Andrews (1993), Andrews and Ploberger (1994), Gregory and Hansen (1996), did some major works in this area. Studies by Nelson and Plosser (1982), Perron (1989), Zivot and Andrews (1992) tested unit root in presence of structural break. Bai (1994, 1997) considered the distributional properties of the break dates.

The second group of studies was an improvement over the first as it was able to detect multiple structural breaks in a financial time series, most importantly endogenous breakpoints. Significant contributions were made by Zivot and Andrews (1992). Perron (1989, 1997b), Bai and Perron (2003), Lumsdaine and Papell (1997) tests for unit root allowing for two breaks in the trend function. Hansen (2001) considers multiple breaks, although he considers the breaks to be exogenously given.

The major breakthrough was the study by Inclan and Tiao (1994), who proposed a test to detect shifts in unconditional variance, that is, the volatility. This test is used extensively in financial time series to identify breaks in volatility (Wilson et al. 1996; Aggarwal et al. 1999; Huang and Yang 2001). This test was later modified by (Sansó et al. 2004) to account for conditional variance as well.

Hsu et al. (1974) proposed in their study a model with non-stationary variance which is subjected to changes. This is probably the first work involving structural

2.3 Detection of Structural Break in Volatility

breaks in variance. Hsu's later works in 1977, 1979, and 1982 were aimed at detecting a single break in variance in a time series. Abraham and Wei (1984) discussed methods of identifying a single structural shift in variance. An improvement came in the study of Baufays and Rasson (1985) who addressed the issue with multiple breakpoints in their paper. Tsay (1988) also discussed ARMA models allowing for outliers and variance changes and proposed a method for detecting the breakpoint in variance. More recently, Cheng (2009) provided an algorithm to detect multiple structural breakpoints for a change in mean as well as a change in variance.

This study does not explicitly incorporate any regime switching model but considers the period between two breaks as a regime. Schaller and Norden (1997) used Markov Switching model to find very strong evidence of regime switch in CRSP value-weighted monthly stock market returns from 1929 to 1989. Marcucci (2005) used a regime switching GARCH model to forecast volatility in S&P500 which is characterized by several regime switches. Structural breaks and regime switch is addressed by Ismail and Isa (2006) who used a SETAR-type model to test structural breaks in Malaysian Ringgit, Singapore Dollar, and Thai Baht.

Theoretically, volatility break dates are structural breaks in variance of a given time series. Structural breaks are often defined as persistent and pronounced macroeconomic shifts in the data generating process. Usually, the probability of observing any structural break increases as we expand the period of study. The methodology used in this chapter is the line of analysis followed by Inclan and Tiao (1994). In the following section, we briefly recapitulate the methodology.

We may start from a simple AR(1) process as that described in (2.1)

$$y_t = \alpha + \rho y_{t-1} + \varepsilon_t$$
$$E\varepsilon_t^2 = \sigma^2 \tag{2.1}$$

Here ε_t is a time series of serially uncorrelated shocks. If the series is stationary, the parameters α, ρ and σ^2 are constant over time. By definition, a structural break occurs if at least one of the parameters changes permanently at some point in time (Hansen 2001). The time point where the parameter changes value is often termed as a "break date". According to Brooks (2002), structural breaks are irreversible in nature. The reasons behind occurrence of structural breaks, however, are not very specified. Economic and non-economic (or even unidentifiable) reasons are equally likely to bring about structural break in volatility. (Valentinyi-Endrész 2004).

2.3.1 Detection of Multiple Structural Breaks in Variance: The ICSS Test

The Iterative Cumulative Sum of Squares (or the ICSS) algorithm by Inclan and Tiao (1994) can very well detect sudden changes in unconditional variance for a stochastic process. Hence, the test is often used to detect multiple shifts in volatility. The algorithm starts from the premise that over an initial period, the time series under consideration displays a stationary variance. The variance changes following a shock to the system and continues to be stationary till it experiences another shock in the future. This process is repeated over time till we identify all the breaks. Structural breaks can effectively capture regime switches (Altissimo and Corradi 2003; Gonzalo and Pitarakis 2002; Valentinyi-Endrész 2004). The different tests for identifying volatility breaks isolate dates where conditional volatility moves from one stationary level to another. The idea is similar to those lying behind the Markov regime switching models, where a system jumps from one volatility regime to another.

2.3.1.1 The Original Model: Breaks in Unconditional Variance

The original model of Inclan and Tiao (1994) are reproduced as follows:

Let $C_k = \sum_{t=1}^{k} a_t^2$, $k = 1, \ldots, T$ is the cumulative sum of squares for a series of independent observations $\{a_t\}$, where $a_t \sim iidN(0, \sigma^2)$ and $t = 1, 2, \ldots, T$, σ^2 is the unconditional variance.

$$
\sigma^2 = \begin{cases}
\tau_0, & 1 < t < \kappa_1 \\
\tau_1, & \kappa_1 < t < \kappa_2 \\
\cdots \\
\tau_{N_T}, & \kappa_{N_T} < t < T
\end{cases} \tag{2.2}
$$

where $1 < \kappa_1 < \kappa_2 < \cdots \kappa_{N_T} < T$ are the breakpoints, that is, where the breaks in variances occur. N_T is the total number of such changes for T observations. Within each interval, the variance is $\tau_j^2, j = 0, 1, \ldots, N_T$

The centralized or normalized cumulative sum of squares is denoted by D_k where

$$
D_k = \frac{C_k}{C_T} - \frac{k}{T} \rightarrow D_0 = D_T = 0 \tag{2.3}
$$

C_T is the sum of squared residuals for the whole sample period.

If there is no volatility shift D_k will oscillate around zero. With a change in variance, it will drift upward or downward and will exhibit a pattern going out of some specified boundaries (provided by a critical value based on the distribution of D_k) with high probability. If at some k, say k^*, the maximum absolute value of D_k, given by $\max_k \left| \sqrt{T/2} D_k \right|$ exceeds the critical value, the null hypothesis of constant variance is rejected and k^* will be regarded as an estimate of the change point. Under variance homogeneity, $\sqrt{T/2} D_k$ behaves like a Brownian bridge asymptotically.

For multiple breakpoints, however, the usefulness of the D_k function is questionable due to "masking effect". To avoid this, Inclan and Tiao designed an

2.3 Detection of Structural Break in Volatility

iterative algorithm that uses successive application of the D_k function at different points in the time series to look for possible shift in volatility.

2.3.1.2 Modified ICSS Test: Breaks in Conditional Variance

The modified ICSS test is reproduced and used in this study. Sansó et al. (1994) found significant size distortions for the ICSS test in presence of excessive kurtosis and conditional heteroscedasticity. This makes original ICSS test invalid in the context of financial time series that are often characterized by fat tails and conditional heteroscedasticity. As a remedial measure, they introduced two tests to explicitly consider the fourth moment properties of the disturbances and the conditional heteroscedasticity.

The first test, or the k_1 test, makes the asymptotic distribution free of nuisance parameters for *iid* zero mean random variables.

$$\kappa_1 = \sup_k \left| T^{-1/2} B_k \right|, \quad k = 1, \ldots, T$$

$$B_k = \frac{C_k - \frac{k}{T} C_T}{\sqrt{\hat{\eta}_4 - \hat{\sigma}^4}}, \quad \hat{\eta}_4 = T^{-1} \sum_{t=1}^{T} \varepsilon_t^4 \text{ and } \hat{\sigma}^4 = T^{-1} C_T \tag{2.4}$$

This statistic is free of any nuisance parameter. The second test, the κ_2 test solves the problems of fat tails and persistent volatility.

$$\kappa_2 = \sup_k \left| T^{-1/2} G_k \right| \tag{2.5}$$

where $G_k = \hat{\omega}_4^{-\frac{1}{2}} (C_k - \frac{k}{T} C_T)$

$\hat{\omega}_4$ is a consistent estimator of ω_4. A nonparametric estimator of ω_4 can be expressed as

$$\hat{\omega}_4 = \frac{1}{T} \sum_{i=1}^{T} (\varepsilon_t^2 - \hat{\sigma}^2)^2 + \frac{2}{T} \sum_{l=1}^{m} \omega(l, m) \sum_{t=1}^{T} (\varepsilon_t^2 - \hat{\sigma}^2)(\varepsilon_{t-1}^2 - \hat{\sigma}^2) \tag{2.6}$$

$\omega(l, m)$ is a lag window, such as Bartlett and defined as $\omega(l, m) = [1 - l/(m + 1)]$. The bandwidth m is chosen by Newey-West (1994) technique. The κ_2 test is more powerful than the original Inclan-Tiao test or even the κ_1 test and is best fit for our purpose.

The use of the above-mentioned tests on our data set identifies the sub-phases mentioned earlier. One point, however, is to be noted while considering these sub-phases. The period of aftermath might be found to be characterized by further fluctuations in the Indian stock market, some of which might even be capable of generating further financial market crisis. However, analysts often consider it too early to call this period another era of financial crisis. This period of financial turmoil and vulnerability should be better treated as aftershocks of the crisis of 2007–2008 than altogether a new eon of crisis. Moreover, the fluctuations in recent years are yet to be comparable to the older ones in terms of their overall devastating impact on the real economy. Our study hence is built particularly around the financial crisis of 2007–2008. And hence, the crisis period and its aftermath are exclusively in terms of this financial crisis.

2.4 Identifying Trends in Indian Stock Market: The Methodology

The latent structure in the market could be best analyzed by using an exploratory factor analysis (EFA). EFA is a simple, nonparametric method for extracting relevant information from large correlated data sets (Hair et al. 2010). It could reduce a complex data set to a lower dimension to reveal the sometimes hidden, simplified structures that often underlie it. In EFA, each variable (X_i) is expressed as a linear combination of underlying factors (F_i). The amount of variance each variable shares with others is called communality. The covariance among variables is described by common factors and a unique factor (U_i) for each variable. Hence,

$$X_i = A_{i1}F_1 + \cdots + A_{im}F_m + V_iU_i \tag{2.7}$$

$$\text{and } F_i = W_{i1}X_1 + \cdots + W_{ik}X_k \tag{2.8}$$

where, A_{i1} is the standardized multiple regression coefficient of variable i on factor j; V_i is the standardized regression coefficient of variable i on unique factor i; m is the number of common factors; W_i's are the factor scores, and k is the number of variables. The unique factors are uncorrelated with each other and with common factors.

The appropriateness of using EFA on a data set could be judged by Bartlett's test of sphericity and the Kaiser-Meyar-Olkin (KMO) measure. The Bartlett's test of sphericity tests the null of population correlation matrix to be an identity matrix. A statistically significant Bartlett statistic indicates the extent of correlation among variables to be sufficient to use EFA. Moreover, KMO measure of sampling adequacy should exceed 0.50 for appropriateness of EFA.

In factor analysis, the variables are grouped according to their correlation so that variables under a particular factor are strongly correlated with each other. When variables are correlated they will share variances among them. A variable's communality is the estimate of its shared variance among the variables represented by a specific factor.

Through appropriate methods, factor scores could be selected so that the first factor explains the largest portion of the total variance. Then a second set, uncorrelated to the first, could be found so that the second factor accounts for most of the residual variance and so on. This chapter uses the Principal Component method where the total variance in data is considered. The method helps when we isolate minimum number of factors accounting for maximum variance in data.

2.4 Identifying Trends in Indian Stock Market: The Methodology

Factors with eigenvalues greater than 1.0 are retained. An eigenvalue represents the amount of variance associated with the factor. Factors with eigenvalues less than one are not better than a single variable, because after standardization, each variable has a variance of 1.0.

Interpretation of factors will require an examination of the factor loadings. A factor loading is the correlation of the variable and the factor. Hence, the squared loading is the variable's total variance accounted by the factor. Thus, a 0.50 loading implies that 25 % of the variance of the variable is explained by the factor. Usually, factor loadings in the range of ±0.30 to ±0.40 are minimally required for interpretation of a structure. Loadings greater than or equal to ±0.50 are practically significant while loadings greater than or equal to ±0.70 imply presence of well-defined structures.

The initial or unrotated factor matrix, however, shows the relationship between the factors and the variables where factor solutions extract factors in the order of their variance extracted. The first factor accounting for the largest amount of variance in the data is a general factor where almost every variable has significant loading. The subsequent factors are based on the residual amount of variance. Such factors are difficult to interpret as a single factor could be related to many variables. Factor rotation provides simpler factor structures that are easier to interpret. With rotation, the reference axes of the factors are rotated about the origin, until some other positions are reached. With factor rotation, variance is re-distributed from the earlier factor to the latter. Effectively, one factor will be significantly correlated with only a few variables and a single variable will have high and significant loading with only one factor. In an orthogonal factor rotation, as the axes are maintained at angles of 90°, the resultant factors will be uncorrelated to each other. Within the orthogonal factor rotation methods, VARIMAX is the most popular method where the sum of variances of the required loading of the factor matrix is maximized. There are, however, oblique factor rotations where the reference axes are not maintained at 90° angles. The resulting factors will not be totally uncorrelated to each other. This chapter will use that method of factor rotation which will fit the data best.

The study then employs Cronbach's alpha as a measure of internal consistency. In theory a high value of alpha is often used as evidence that the items measure an underlying (or latent) construct. Cronbach's alpha, however, is not a statistical test. It is a coefficient of reliability or consistency.

The standardized Cronbach's alpha could be written as: $a = \frac{N.\bar{c}}{\bar{v}+(N-1).\bar{c}}$

Here N is the number of items (here markets); $\bar{c}$ is the average inter-item covariance among the items and $\bar{v}$ is the average variance. From the formula, it is clear that an increase in the number of items increases Cronbach's alpha. Additionally, if the average inter-item correlation increases, Cronbach's alpha increases as well (holding the number of items constant). This study uses Cronbach's alpha to check how closely related a set of markets are as a group and whether they indeed form a 'group' among themselves.

2.5 Trends and Latent Structure in Indian Stock Market: Bombay Stock Exchange

1. *Trends over the entire period: 2005 January to 2012 September*

The study starts from an analysis of correlation among the different indexes. Table 2.1 suggests presence of statistically significant correlation among market as well as sectoral returns over the entire study period.

To justify the use of EFA over the chosen data set we consider the KMO and Bartlett's tests for data adequacy. The KMO measure of sampling adequacy takes a value of 0.873 and Bartlett's test statistic of sphericity is significant at one percent level of significance implying validity of using EFA on our data set.

Based on eigenvalue a single factor (eigenvalue 8.784) is extracted that explains 73.2 % of total variability. The single factor contains all the indexes that are highly loaded in that factor. The Cronbach's alpha stands at 0.9631 and declines with exclusion of each index. This makes the extracted structure a valid one (Table 2.2).

The presence of a single structure implies the presence of a single dominant trend in the market. All the sectors and the market move in similar fashion and direction (as reflected in their positive loadings on the factor). The indexes are highly correlated and together they reflect a distinct and broad market trend. The detailed analysis of such broad, dominant trend could be of further interest.

Analysis of market trend: use of factor score

In EFA, factors represent latent constructs. From a practical standpoint, researchers often estimate scores on a latent construct (i.e., factor scores) and use them instead of the set of items that load on that factor. While constructing a factor score, researchers could use the sum or average of the scores on items loading on that factor. However, the procedure could be refined and made statistically acceptable by using the information contained in the factor solution. The problem with such elementary construction of factor score is that simple average uses only the information that the set of items load on a given factor. The process fails if items have different loadings on the factor. In such cases, some items, with relatively high loadings, are better measures of the underlying factor (i.e., more highly correlated with the factor) than others. Therefore, construction of 'good' factor scores requires attaching higher weights to items with high loadings and vice versa. The weights that are used to combine scores on observed items to form factor scores could be obtained through some form of least squares regression. Thus, the factor scores obtained serve as estimates of their corresponding unobserved counterparts.

The use of EFA on our data set extracts a single factor that could be thought of as representing the broad trend in the stock market. However, the stock market trend could not be properly or effectively analyzed until and unless we could get some proxy for this trend. Individual items in the factors (the market index and all the sectoral indexes) could be analyzed separately but the process will provide us

Table 2.1 Correlation matrix among BSE index returns (2005–2012)

	AUTO	BANK	SENSEX	CD	CG	FMCG	HC	IT	PSU	METAL	ONG
BSE AUTO											
BSE BANK	0.727										
BSE SENSEX	0.822	0.892									
BSE CD	0.660	0.611	0.0681								
BSE CG	0.747	0.780	0.866	0.664							
BSE FMCG	0.607	0.557	0.690	0.527	0.564						
BSE HC	0.687	0.639	0.744	0.631	0.668	0.613					
BSE IT	0.575	0.585	0.758	0.501	0.577	0.488	0.557				
BSE PSU	0.770	0.824	0.881	0.701	0.821	0.622	0.734	0.569			
BSE METAL	0.749	0.731	0.847	0.672	0.757	0.585	0.680	0.589	0.818		
BSE ONG	0.701	0.726	0.883	0.610	0.736	0.572	0.667	0.590	0.833	0.766	
BSE POWER	0.763	0.792	0.885	0.691	0.887	0.610	0.713	0.587	0.899	0.803	0.796

All correlations are statistically significant at 1 % level of significance

Table 2.2 Factor loadings in the single factor extracted: entire period

BSE AUTO	0.862	BSE HC	0.812
BSE BANK	0.871	BSE IT	0.714
BSE SENSEX	0.974	BSE PSU	0.930
BSE CD	0.773	BSE METAL	0.882
BSE CG	0.891	BSE ONG	0.871
BSE FMCG	0.719	BSE POWER	0.926

with hardly any insight regarding the broad trend. We could instead construct the factor score for our single extracted factor. These factor scores then could serve as a proxy for the latent structure of the market. That is where the study moves next.

The movement or behavior of market trends (given by the factor scores), henceforth described as the *stock market* is depicted in Fig. 2.1. As is evident from the diagram, the stock market movement is highly volatile, characterized by the presence of volatility clustering where periods of high (low) volatility are followed by periods of high (low) volatility. However, from the simple plot it is difficult to form any idea regarding the trends and nature of movements properly.

The trend could be better analyzed if it is possible to bring out the nature of the cycle inherent in the series. For this purpose, the study uses the method of band pass (frequency) filter. The band pass (frequency) filters are used to isolate the cyclical component of a time series by specifying a range for its duration. The band pass filter is a linear filter that takes a two-sided weighted moving average of the data where cycles in a "band", given by a specified lower and upper bound, are "passed" through, or extracted, and the remaining cycles are "filtered" out. To use a band pass filter, we have to first specify the 'periods' to 'pass through. The periods are defined in terms of two numbers (P_L and P_U) based on the units of the frequency of the series used. There are different band pass filters that differ in their treatment of the moving average. The study uses the full sample asymmetric filter, where the weights on the leads and lags are allowed to differ. The asymmetric filter is time-varying with the weights both depending on the data and changing for each observation. The study uses the Christiano–Fitzgerald (CF) form of this filter. As a rule of thumb, P_L and P_U are set as 1.5 and 8 years for yearly data. The ranges for daily data should be adjusted accordingly. The series is found to be level stationary using Augmented Dickey Fuller test statistic (null hypothesis of unit root is

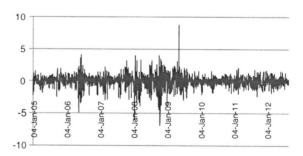

Fig. 2.1 Movements in factor scores, BSE (2005–2012)

2.5 Trends and Latent Structure in Indian Stock Market: Bombay Stock Exchange

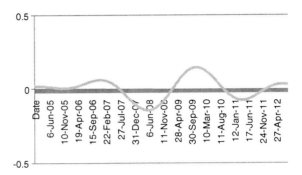

Fig. 2.2 Cycle in the BSE return (2005–2012)

rejected at one percent level of significance). We chose to de-trend the data before filtering. The cycle is depicted in Fig. 2.2.

The return-cycle for the stock market enables us to identify the ups and downs in BSE. The *stock market* as a whole experiences a boom during the phases namely, 2006–2007, 2009–2010, and since early 2012. The market as a whole slides down from its peak over the periods namely, 2007–2008 and 2010–2011. Our analysis is concentrated around the first cycle.

The trend is further analyzed through an examination of the risk-return relationship in the market as a whole. The variance of a series could serve as a good proxy for the risk of the series. As is suggested by the simple plot of the *stock market* return, the series is characterized by volatility clustering or volatility pooling. Moreover the series is negatively skew (skewness −0.23), highly peaked (kurtosis 6.65), and non-normal. Such a series is best analyzed by an appropriate GARCH family model and risk for such a series is proxied best by its conditional variance.

The *stock market* is modeled best by Exponential GARCH (EGARCH) model, an asymmetric GARCH model of order (1, 1). The study uses the version of the model first proposed by Nelson in 1991. The EGARCH (1, 1) model can be specified as:

$$\log(\sigma_t^2) = \omega + \alpha(|z_{t-1}| - E(|z_{t-1}|)) + \gamma z_{t-1} + \beta \log(\sigma_{t-1}^2); \text{ where } \varepsilon_{t-1} = \sigma_{t-1} z_{t-1} \quad (2.9)$$

The dependent variable is not the conditional variance, but rather the log of conditional variance. Hence the leverage effect is exponential rather than quadratic in the EGARCH model. The EGARCH model overcomes the most important limitation of the GARCH model by incorporating the leverage effect. If $\alpha > 0$ and $\gamma = 0$, the innovation in $\log(\sigma_t^2)$ is positive (negative) when z_{t-1} is larger (smaller) than its expected value. And if $\alpha = 0$ and $\gamma < 0$, the innovation in $\log(\sigma_t^2)$ is positive (negative) when z_{t-1} is negative (positive). Another significant improvement of the EGARCH process is that it contains no inequality constraint, and by parameterizing the $\log(\sigma_t^2)$ can take negative value so there are fewer restrictions on the model. Lastly, the EGARCH process can capture volatility persistence quite effectively. $\log(\sigma_t^2)$ can easily be checked for volatility

Table 2.3 Application of EGARCH model on factor score for BSE (2005–2012)

Dependent variable: factor score for BSE (2005–2012)

Method: ML—ARCH (Marquardt)—student's t distribution

Included observations: 1909

Convergence achieved after 23 iterations

Presample variance: backcast (parameter = 0.7)

LOG(GARCH) = C(1) + C(2)*ABS(RESID(−1)/@SQRT(GARCH(−1))) + C(3) *RESID(−1)/@SQRT(GARCH(−1)) + C(4)*LOG(GARCH(−1))

	Variance equation			
	Coefficient	Std. Error	z-Statistic	Prob.
C(1)	−0.18787	0.023173	−8.10761	5.16E-16
C(2)	0.226826	0.028853	7.861378	3.80E-15
C(3)	−0.11943	0.017101	−6.98381	2.87E-12
C(4)	0.961732	0.007329	131.2155	0
T-DIST. DOF	7.678726	0.986114	7.786851	6.87E-15
R-squared	1.11E-15	Mean dependent var		−4.71E-08
Adjusted R-squared	−0.0021	S.D. dependent var		1
S.E. of regression	1.00105	Akaike info criterion		2.433343
Sum squared resid	1908	Schwarz criterion		2.447891
Log likelihood	−2,317.63	Hannan-Quinn criter.		2.438697
Durbin–Watson stat	1.804131			

persistence by looking at the stationarity and ergodicity conditions. However, the EGARCH model is also not free from its drawbacks. This model is difficult to use for there is no analytic form for the volatility term structure.

As is suggested by Table 2.3, the *stock market* is characterized by asymmetric response of volatility toward positive and negative announcements in the market. The market reacts more toward the negative news than toward the good news.

The conditional volatility for the series is saved and depicted in Fig. 2.3.

The conditional variance, after de-trending, exhibits significant cyclical pattern (Fig. 2.4).

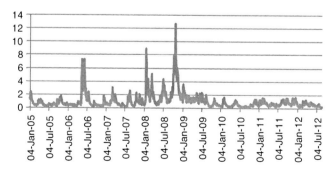

Fig. 2.3 BSE conditional variance (2005–2012)

2.5 Trends and Latent Structure in Indian Stock Market: Bombay Stock Exchange

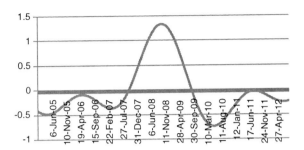

Fig. 2.4 Cycle in the factor score BSE conditional variance (2005–2012)

The conditional volatility has been significantly higher during the period of financial crisis of 2007–2008. The two other peaks are not at all significant compared to this peak. Thus, although the return cyclebrings out two significant peaks in BSE return, conditional variance cycle rules out one and suggests presence of a single high-volatile period in the market. The peak of 2010–2011 is not associated with a very high volatility. This justifies our choice of financial crisis of 2007–2008 as the most significant financial crisis of recent years. The cycle of 2010–2012 is yet to be designated as a true financial crisis. Interestingly, the nature of cycle of conditional variance is completely opposite to the cyclical nature of the return series. Return peaks are always associated with low conditional variance or conditional variance slumps. This is further analyzed and depicted in Fig. 2.4. The nature of time-varying conditional correlation between stock market return and conditional variance brings out the negative relationship between risk and return in the market.

The conditional correlation has been computed using a multivariate GARCH technique that models the variance–covariance matrix of a financial time series. This section makes use of Diagonal Vector GARCH (VECH) model of Bollerslev et al. (1988). In a Diagonal VECH model the variance–covariance matrix of stock market returns is allowed to vary over time. This model is particularly useful, unlike the BEKK model of Baba et al. (1990), with more than two variables in the conditional correlation matrix (Scherrer and Ribarits 2007). However, it is often difficult to guarantee a positive semi-definite conditional variance–covariance matrix in a VECH model (Engel and Kroner 1993; Brooks and Henry 2000). Following the methodology of Karunanayake et al. (2008) this study avoids this problem by using the unconditional residual variance as the pre-sample conditional variance. This is likely to ensure positive semi-definite variance–covariance matrix in a diagonal VECH model. Since, we are more interested in volatility co-movement and spill over, the mean equation of the estimated diagonal VECH model contains only the constant term. In the n dimension variance–covariance matrix, H, the diagonal terms will represent the variance and the non-diagonal terms will represent the covariances. In other words, in

$$H_t = \begin{matrix} h_{11t} & \cdots & h_{1nt} \\ \cdots & \cdots & \cdots \\ h_{n1t} & \cdots & h_{nnt} \end{matrix}$$

h_{iit} is the conditional variance of 'ith market in time t; h_{ijt} is the conditional covariance between the ith and jth market in period t ($i \neq j$). The conditional variance depends on the squared lagged residuals and conditional covariance depends on the cross lagged residuals and lagged covariances of the other series (Karunanayake et al. 2008). The model could be represented as:

$$\text{VECH}(H_t) = C + A.\text{VECH}(\varepsilon_{t-1}\varepsilon'_{t-1}) + B.\text{VECH}(H_{t-1}) \qquad (2.10)$$

A and B are $\frac{N(N+1)}{2} \times \frac{N(N+1)}{2}$ parameter matrices. C is $\frac{N(N+1)}{2}$ vector of constant. a_{ii} in matrix A, that is the diagonal elements show the own spillover effect. This is the impact of own past innovations on present volatility. The cross diagonal terms (a_{ij}, $i \neq j$) show the impact of pat innovation in one market on the present volatility of other markets. Similarly, b_{ii} in matrix B shows the impact of own past volatility on present volatility. Likewise, b_{ij} represents cross volatility spill over or the impact of past volatility of the ith market on the present volatility of jth market. For our purpose, a_{ij}'s and b_{ij}'s are more important.

As pointed out by Karunanayake et al. (2008) an important issue in estimating a diagonal VECH model is the number of parameters to be estimated. To solve the problem, Bollerslev et al. (1988) suggested use of a diagonal form of A and B. A related issue is to ensure the positive semi-definiteness of the variance–covariance matrix. The condition is easily satisfied if all of the parameters in A, B, and C are positive with a positive initial conditional variance–covariance matrix. Bollerslev et al. (1988) suggested some restrictions to impose that have been followed by Karunanayake et al. (2008). They used maximum likelihood function to generate these parameter estimates by imposing some restriction on the initial value. If θ be the parameter for a sample of T observations, the log likelihood function will be:

$$T(\theta) = \sum_{t=1}^{T} l_r(\theta), \quad \text{where } l_t(\theta) = \frac{N}{2}\ln(2\pi) - \frac{1}{2}ln|H_t| - \frac{1}{2}\epsilon'_t H_t^{-1}\epsilon_t \qquad (2.11)$$

The presample values of θ can be set to be equal to their expected value of zero (Bollerslev et al. 1988). The Ljung Box test statistic could further be used to test for remaining ARCH effects. For a stationary time series of T observations and a multivariate process of order (p, q) the Ljung Box test statistic is given as:

$$Q = T^2 \sum_{j=1}^{s} (T-j)^{-1}tj\left\{ C_{Y_t}^{-1}(0)C_{Y_t}(j)C_{Y_t}^{-1}(0)C'_{Y_t}(j) \right\} \qquad (2.12)$$

Y_t is VECH (y_t, y'_t), $C_{Y_t}(j)$ is the sample autocovariance matrix of order j, s is the number of lags used, T is the number of observations. For large sample, the test statistic is distributed as a χ^2 under the null hypothesis of no remaining ARCH effect.

A multivariate GARCH of appropriate order has been estimated for the data on factor scores for BSE return and BSE conditional variance and the conditional correlation values have been saved. The movement in this conditional correlation

2.5 Trends and Latent Structure in Indian Stock Market: Bombay Stock Exchange

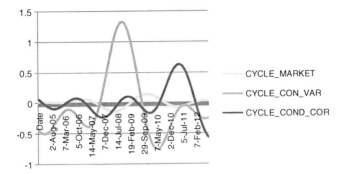

Fig. 2.5 Return-risk relationship BSE (2005–2012)

reflects the risk-return relationship in the context of BSE. During most of the time period, particularly during the financial crisis of 2007–2008, risk and return had been perfectly negatively correlated (correlation coefficient = −1). For only a short period of time, risk and return was perfectly positively correlated (correlation coefficient = +1). This suggests the presence of dominantly negative (perfect) risk-return relationship in BSE. More interestingly, correlation coefficient was either +1 or −1. Only for a short period of time (during August 2010 to January 2012) correlation coefficient remained positive and fluctuated. The characteristics in conditional correlation could further be traced in the cycle in conditional correlation (Fig. 2.5).

The analysis of overall market trend would now be supplemented by analyses of market trend before and after the crisis.

2. *The trends in the pre-crisis period: 2005 January to 2008 January*

The analysis of trends in the market in the pre-crisis period starts from identification of latent structure in the market.

Table 2.4 suggests presence of statistically significant correlation among market as well as sectoral returns during the pre-crisis. The correlation coefficients are more or less the same in magnitude compared to those for the entire period.

The use of EFA over the pre-crisis data set is further justified by the favorable values of the KMO measure of sampling adequacy and Bartlett's tests for data adequacy. The KMO measure of sampling adequacy takes a value of 0.885 and Bartlett's test statistic of sphericity is significant at one percent level of significance implying validity of using EFA on the pre-crisis data set.

On the basis of eigenvalue a single factor (eigenvalue 8.908) is extracted that explains 74.2 % of total variability. Both the eigenvalue and the total variability explained by the single factor extracted are higher than those obtained for the *entire period*. Once again, the single factor contains all the indexes that are highly loaded in that factor. The Cronbach's alpha stands at 0.9650 (which is higher than the *entire period*) and declines with exclusion of each index. This makes the extracted structure, once again a valid one (Table 2.5).

Table 2.4 Correlation matrix among BSE index returns (2005–2008)

	AUTO	BANK	SENSEX	CD	CG	FMCG	HC	IT	PSU	METAL	ONG
BSE AUTO											
BSE BANK	0.693										
BSE SENSEX	0.857	0.842									
BSE CD	0.691	0.541	0.656								
BSE CG	0.769	0.693	0.850	0.633							
BSE FMCG	0.686	0.562	0.753	0.569	0.638						
BSE HC	0.760	0.659	0.802	0.670	0.724	0.670					
BSE IT	0.650	0.572	0.785	0.507	0.606	0.495	0.606				
BSE PSU	0.812	0.794	0.897	0.692	0.812	0.685	0.787	0.610			
BSE METAL	0.765	0.673	0.837	0.648	0.752	0.663	0.728	0.592	0.834		
BSE ONG	0.747	0.678	0.876	0.612	0.728	0.657	0.718	0.603	0.869	0.760	
BSE POWER	0.780	0.716	0.855	0.660	0.867	0.652	0.750	0.588	0.894	0.794	0.783

All correlations are statistically significant at 1 % level of significance

2.5 Trends and Latent Structure in Indian Stock Market: Bombay Stock Exchange

Table 2.5 Factor loadings in the single factor extracted: pre-crisis period

BSE AUTO	0.894	BSE HC	0.861
BSE BANK	0.818	BSE IT	0.733
BSE SENSEX	0.971	BSE PSU	0.943
BSE CD	0.760	BSE METAL	0.879
BSE CG	0.882	BSE ONG	0.879
BSE FMCG	0.776	BSE POWER	0.909

The presence of a single structure implies the presence of a single dominant trend in the market even in the *pre-crisis* period. All the sectors and the market move in similar fashion and direction (as reflected in their positive loadings on the factor). The indexes are highly correlated and together they reflect a distinct and broad market trend. The detailed analysis of such broad, dominant trend in the *pre-crisis* period would be our further area of analysis.

Analysis of market trend in pre-crisis period: use of factor score

The use of EFA on our *pre-crisis* data set extracts a single factor that could be thought of as representing the broad trend in the stock market in the *pre-crisis* period. However, this stock market trend cannot be properly or effectively analyzed until and unless we could get some proxy for this trend. Just like the previous case, we have constructed the factor score for our single extracted factor for the *pre-crisis* period. These factor scores then serve as a proxy for the latent structure of the *pre-crisis* market.

The movement or behavior of market trends (given by the factor scores), henceforth described as the *stock market in pre-crisis period*, is depicted in Fig. 2.6. As is evident from the diagram, the stock market movement is highly volatile, characterized by the presence of volatility clustering where periods of high (low) volatility are followed by periods of high (low) volatility. However, from the simple plot it is difficult to form any idea regarding the trends and nature of movements properly. The trend in the *pre-crisis period* resembles that for the *entire Period*.

The trend could be better analyzed if it is possible to bring out the nature of the cycle inherent in the series. The cycle is generated once again using the method of band pass (frequency) filter in its CF form. The *pre-crisis* series is found to be level stationary using Augmented Dickey Fuller test statistic (null hypothesis of unit root is rejected at one percent level of significance). We chose to de-trend the data before filtering. The cycle is depicted in Fig. 2.7.

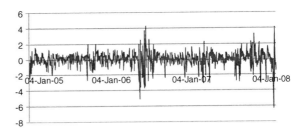

Fig. 2.6 Movements in factor scores, BSE (2005–2008)

Fig. 2.7 Cycle in the BSE return (2005–2008)

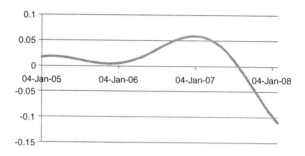

The cycle for the stock market enables us to identify the ups and downs in returns in the BSE in the *pre-crisis* period. As suggested by our earlier analysis, the *stockmarket* as a whole experienced a boom during the phases namely, 2006–2007, 2009–2010, and since early 2012. The market as a whole slides down from its peak over the periods namely, 2007–2008 and 2010–2011. An analysis of the *pre-crisis* period return shows distinct cycle that is different from the cycle that we obtained from our earlier analysis of the entire period. If we could take the *pre-crisis* period separately, and not as a part of the entire period, a small peak could be traced during the period of 2005–2006. This peak was not very prominent in the cycle for the entire period. There has been another significant peak in the *pre-crisis* period that could be traced during the period of 2007–2008. The market in the *pre-crisis* period started declining just toward the end of the period namely in January 2008.

The trend is further analyzed through examination of the risk-return relationship in the market as a whole. The variance of a series could serve as a good proxy for the risk of the series. As is suggested by the simple plot of the *stock market* return, the series is characterized by volatility clustering or volatility pooling. Moreover, the series is negatively skew (skewness −0.25), highly peaked (kurtosis 8.65), and non-normal. Such a series is best analyzed by an appropriate GARCH family model and risk for such a series is proxied best by its conditional variance.

The *stock market* is modeled best by EGARCH, an asymmetric GARCH model of order (1, 1, 1). As is suggested by Table 2.6, the *stock market* in the *pre-crisis* period is characterized by asymmetric response of volatility toward positive and negative announcements in the market. The market reacts more toward the negative news than toward the good news.

The conditional volatility for the *pre-crisis* series is saved and depicted in Fig. 2.8.

The conditional variance, after de-trending, exhibits significant cyclical pattern. The conditional volatility has been significantly higher during the period of 2005–2006. The conditional volatility was significantly lower during mid-2007. However, just before the crisis was to set in, conditional volatility started mounting. Thus risk in a market (given by the conditional variance) starts escalating as the market approaches a crisis. The risk-return relationship in the market is further analyzed and depicted in Fig. 2.9. The nature of time-varying conditional

2.5 Trends and Latent Structure in Indian Stock Market: Bombay Stock Exchange

Table 2.6 Application of EGARCH model on factor score for BSE (2005–2008)

Dependent Variable: Return in the *pre-crisis* period
Method: ML—ARCH (Marquardt)—Student's t distribution
Included observations: 771 after adjustments
Convergence achieved after 20 iterations
Presample variance: backcast (parameter = 0.7)
LOG(GARCH) = C(1) + C(2)*ABS(RESID(−1)/@SQRT(GARCH(−1))) + C(3)*RESID(−1)/@SQRT(GARCH(−1))) + C(4)*LOG(GARCH(−1))

	Variance equation			
	Coefficient	Std. error	z-statistic	Prob.
C(1)	−0.230081	0.051685	−4.451629	0
C(2)	0.252992	0.062029	4.078632	0
C(3)	−0.235055	0.039617	−5.933215	0
C(4)	0.882705	0.024141	36.56491	0
T-DIST. DOF	6.19328	1.366128	4.533454	0
R-squared	0	Mean dependent var		0.000391
Adjusted R-squared	−0.005222	S.D. dependent var		1.00059
S.E. of regression	1.003199	Akaike info criterion		2.424167
Sum squared resid	770.9089	Schwarz criterion		2.454307
Log likelihood	−929.5162	Hannan-Quinn criter.		2.435765
Durbin–Watson stat	1.780743			

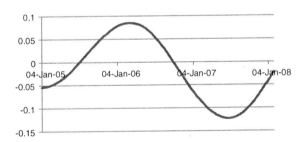

Fig. 2.8 Cycle in the factor score BSE conditional variance (2005–2008)

correlation brings out the presence of a positive relationship between risk and return in the market. While the correlation fluctuates, it started declining since mid-2007 and approached zero toward the beginning of the crisis.

Hence, the analysis of *pre-crisis* period reveals few notable characteristics of Indian stock market:

- Indian stock market is dominated by a "single" trend where all the sectors and the market move together. The trend in the pre-crisis period is stronger than the 'average' (the trend for the entire period) market trend.
- The entire stock market is characterized by significant volatility with volatility clustering.

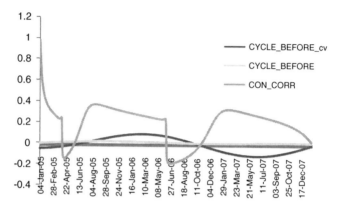

Fig. 2.9 Return-risk relationship BSE (2005–2008)

- Asymmetric response of volatility toward good and bad news where volatility responds more toward bad news. The leverage effect is more pronounced in the *pre-crisis* period (coefficient = −0.23) compared to the entire period (−0.11)
- Returns start falling and risks start mounting as the market approaches a crisis.
- Market is mostly characterized by a positive risk-return relationship. However, the correlation coefficient between risk and return starts declining as the market approaches crisis. Just before the crisis sets in, the correlation coefficient becomes zero.

3. *The trends in the post-crisis period: 2008 February to 2012 September*

The analysis of market trend in the post-crisis period starts from identification of latent structure in the market. Table 2.7 suggests presence of statistically significant correlation among market as well sectoral returns during the post-crisis period. The correlation coefficients are more or less the same in magnitude compared to those for the *entire* and *pre-crisis* period.

The use of EFA over the post-crisis period data set is once again justified by the favorable values of the KMO measure of sampling adequacy and Bartlett's tests for data adequacy. The KMO measure of sampling adequacy takes a value of 0.866 and Bartlett's test statistic of sphericity is significant at one percent level of significance implying validity of using EFA on the post-crisis data set.

On the basis of eigenvalue a single factor (eigenvalue 8.740) is extracted that could explains 72.83 % of total variability. Both the eigenvalue and the total variability explained by the single factor extracted are lower than those obtained for the *entire period* as well as for the *pre-crisis* period. Once again, the single factor contains all the indexes that are highly loaded in that factor. The Cronbach's alpha stands at 0.9625 (which is lower than those obtained for the *entire period* as well as for the *pre-crisis period*) and declines with exclusion of each index. This makes the extracted structure, once again a valid one (Table 2.8).

Table 2.7 Correlation matrix among BSE index returns (2008–2012)

	AUTO	BANK	SENSEX	CD	CG	FMCG	HC	IT	PSU	METAL	ONG
BSE AUTO											
BSE BANK	0.747										
BSE SENSEX	0.807	0.914									
BSE CD	0.642	0.652	0.698								
BSE CG	0.739	0.817	0.873	0.683							
BSE FMCG	0.559	0.571	0.667	0.499	0.532						
BSE HC	0.643	0.646	0.725	0.607	0.652	0.563					
BSE IT	0.537	0.592	0.747	0.501	0.566	0.493	0.536				
BSE PSU	0.745	0.847	0.878	0.707	0.832	0.578	0.698	0.549			
BSE METAL	0.742	0.760	0.853	0.687	0.759	0.539	0.657	0.588	0.810		
BSE ONG	0.678	0.750	0.887	0.609	0.739	0.524	0.644	0.585	0.815	0.768	
BSE POWER	0.756	0.831	0.902	0.710	0.899	0.589	0.698	0.589	0.904	0.809	0.802

All correlations are statistically significant at 1 % level of significance

Table 2.8 Factor loadings in the single factor extracted: post-crisis period

BSE AUTO	0.844	BSE HC	0.787
BSE BANK	0.900	BSE IT	0.705
BSE SENSEX	0.977	BSE PSU	0.924
BSE CD	0.781	BSE METAL	0.883
BSE CG	0.897	BSE ONG	0.867
BSE FMCG	0.686	BSE POWER	0.936

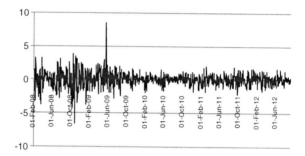

Fig. 2.10 Movements in factor scores, BSE (2008–2012)

The presence of a single structure implies the presence of a single dominant trend in the market even in the *post-crisis* period. All the sectors and the market move in similar fashion and direction (as reflected in their positive loadings on the factor). The indexes are highly correlated and together they reflect a distinct and broad market trend. The detailed analysis of such broad, dominant trend in the *post-crisis* period would be our further area of analysis.

Analysis of market trend in post-crisis period: use of factor score

The use of EFA on our *post-crisis* data set extracts a single factor that could be thought of as representing the broad trend in the stock market in the *post-crisis* period. However, to analyze this stock market trend properly and effectively, we need to get some proxy for this trend. Just like the previous two cases, we have constructed the factor score for our single extracted factor for the *post-crisis* period. These factor scores then serve as a proxy for the latent structure of the *post-crisis* market.

The movement or behavior of market trends (given by the factor scores), henceforth described as the *stock market in post-crisis period*, is depicted in Fig. 2.10. As it is evident from the diagram, the stock market movement is highly volatile, characterized by the presence of volatility clustering where periods of high (low) volatility are followed by periods of high (low) volatility. However, from the simple plot it is difficult to form any idea regarding the trends and nature of movements properly. The trend in the *post-crisis period* resembles those for the *entire* as well as the *pre-crisis periods*. The volatility is significantly higher during the period of February 2008 to March 2009: the period when stock market was sliding.

2.5 Trends and Latent Structure in Indian Stock Market: Bombay Stock Exchange

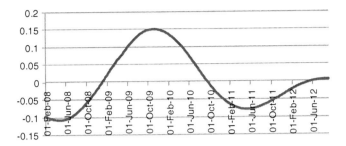

Fig. 2.11 Cycle in the BSE (2008–2012)

The trend could be better analyzed if it is possible to bring out the nature of the cycle inherent in the series. The cycle in the *post-crisis* market return movement is depicted in Fig. 2.11. The cycle is generated once again using the same method of band pass (frequency) filter in its CF form. The *post-crisis* series is found to be level stationary using Augmented Dickey Fuller test statistic (null hypothesis of unit root is rejected at one percent level of significance). We chose to de-trend the data before filtering. The cycle is depicted in Fig. 2.11.

The cycle for the stock market enables us to identify the ups and downs in returns in the BSE in the *post-crisis* period. The return was lower during the period of 2008–2009, the period of crisis. Return increased gradually over the year of 2009 and reached a peak in November 2009. Return dipped since then and made a gradual, but not very significant improvement since mid-2011. The trend is further analyzed through examination of the risk-return relationship in the market as a whole in the *post-crisis* period. The variance of a series could serve as a good proxy for the risk of the series. As is suggested by the simple plot of the *stock market* return, the series is characterized by volatility clustering or volatility pooling. Moreover, the series is negatively skew (skewness −0.26), highly peaked (kurtosis 7.65), and non-normal. Such a series is best analyzed by an appropriate GARCH family model and risk for such a series is proxied best by its conditional variance.

The *stock market* is modeled best by EGARCH, an asymmetric GARCH model of order (1, 1). As is suggested by Table 2.9 the *stock market* in the *post-crisis* period is characterized by asymmetric response of volatility toward positive and negative announcements in the market. The market reacts more toward the negative news than toward the good news.

The conditional volatility for the *post-crisis* series is saved and depicted in Fig. 2.12.

The conditional variance, after de-trending, exhibits significant cyclical pattern. The conditional volatility has been significantly higher during the period of 2008–2009. The conditional volatility was significantly lower during late 2009–2011. Thus, volatility and hence risk, remained significantly higher during the period of crisis. The risk-return relationship in the market is further analyzed and depicted in Fig. 2.13. The nature of time-varying conditional correlation

Table 2.9 Application of EGARCH model on factor score for BSE (2008–2012)

Dependent variable: return in the *post-crisis* period
Method: ML—ARCH (Marquardt)—Student's t distribution
Included observations: 1137
Convergence achieved after 28 iterations
Presample variance: backcast (parameter = 0.7)
LOG(GARCH) = C(1) + C(2)*ABS(RESID(−1)/@SQRT(GARCH(-1))) + C(3) *RESID(−1)/@SQRT(GARCH(−1)) + C(4)*LOG(GARCH(−1))

	Variance equation			
	Coefficient	Std. error	z-statistic	Prob.
C(1)	−0.14429	0.025556	−5.64629	0
C(2)	0.17386	0.03189	5.451858	0
C(3)	−0.08342	0.017128	−4.87047	0
C(4)	0.983369	0.005623	174.8838	0
T-DIST. DOF	11.02265	1.913501	5.760461	0
R-squared	0	Mean dependent var		−1.76E-08
Adjusted R-squared	−0.00353	S.D. dependent var		1
S.E. of regression	1.001765	Akaike info criterion		2.422552
Sum squared resid	1136	Schwarz criterion		2.444699
Log likelihood	−1372.22	Hannan–Quinn criter.		2.430917
Durbin–Watson stat	1.814822			

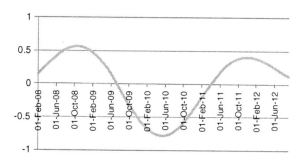

Fig. 2.12 Cycle in the factor score BSE conditional variance (2008–2012)

brings out the presence of a positive relationship between risk and return in the market. During the period of 2008, the correlation coefficient was negative, implying a negative risk-return relationship in the market. Since then the risk-return relationship has been mostly positive, with some exceptions during 2010–2011 and during late 2012. The conditional correlation cycle in the *post-crisis* period is, however, smoother compared to that in the *pre-crisis* period.

Hence, the analysis of *post-crisis* period reveals few notable characteristics of Indian stock market:

2.5 Trends and Latent Structure in Indian Stock Market: Bombay Stock Exchange

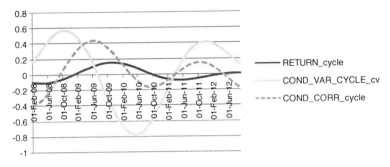

Fig. 2.13 Return-risk relationship BSE (2008–2012)

- Indian stock market is dominated by a "single" trend where all the sectors and the market move together. The trend in the post-crisis period is weaker than the 'average' (the trend for the entire period) market trend as well as the trend in the pre-crisis period.
- The market is characterized by significant volatility with volatility clustering.
- Asymmetric response of volatility toward good and bad news where volatility responds more toward bad news. The leverage effect is less pronounced in the *post-crisis* period (coefficient = −0.08) compared to that in the entire period (−0.11) and in the pre-crisis period (−0.23).
- Returns start falling and risks start mounting as the market plunges into a crisis.
- Market is mostly characterized by a positive risk-return relationship. However, the correlation coefficient between risk and return starts declining and becomes negative as the market dips into crisis.

The trends in BSE: Any 'Signal' to frame profitable trading strategy?

Over the past 8 years, the Indian stock market, as represented by the BSE, is dominated by a "single" trend where all the sectors and the market move together. The latent structure of the market is constructed of all the sectors and the market Index. The structure has remained unchanged over the past 8 years and has been independent of the cycles in the economy. Moreover, the trend in the post-crisis period is weaker than the 'average' (the trend for the entire period) market trend, whereas the trend in the pre-crisis period is stronger than the 'average'. This is revealed by the EFA where the single factor extracted could account for more variability (as given by the values of the Eigenvectors) in the pre-crisis period than for the post-crisis period. Further analysis of eigenvalue and eigenvector composition might provide us with significant signals that might be useful as an indicator of future events. For example, if a unique eigenvector composition is consistently observed before a market crash or period of market growth, then this unique eigenvector provides a signal that can be responded to in the future. As the economy passes through different stages, and market forces change, the eigenvectors might be expected to change to describe the new situation. Thus, an analysis of trends in Eigenvector might help us identify pattern and trend in market

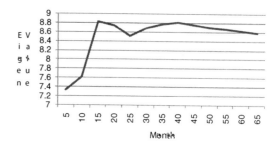

Fig. 2.14 Nature of eigenvalue for BSE (2005–2012)

movements. This in turn might help investors design strategies that would reduce risk and increase gains.

As suggested by our earlier analysis, the market is dominated by a single trend. The single eigenvalue, however, is changing from month to month (Fig. 2.14). The fraction of market variation captured by the first eigenvector thus changes over time. The movements are sometime marked by sharp changes.

Starting from January 2005, eigenvalue increases sharply over the first 15 months. It then falls gradually and reaches a slump during the 25th month. The following months (25th to 40th) witnessed a moderate rise in eigenvalue. The 45th to 65th months witnessed a fall in eigenvalue. The movement in the eigenvalue might indicate the fact that the periods between 0th and 10th month and between 25th and 40th month might be associated with some significant market event so that a larger portion of market variability is being captured by the first (in this context, the single) eigenvector. Thus, when the market experiences or passes through some 'extra-ordinary' events, some 'unique' or 'special' trend persists in the market. As the economy reverts back to its 'normal' state this 'special' trend weakens in the sense that the variability captured by the first factor declines steadily. For investors this information might be extremely useful in designing profitable trading strategy. To be more specific, if it is possible to identify when this special trend would set in or how long it would last, investors might be able to design strategies to make profit out of market movements. The movements in the first factor eigenvalue reveal few more observations. The eigenvalue increases during the periods of recovery and reaches maximum just before the peak. During a stable period, however, the eigenvalue falls or reaches a plateau. Therefore, the 'special' trend persists during the phases of recovery and weakens during the periods of recession or stability. The market crash could be predicted from a high eigenvalue of the first factor and high eigenvalue could be associated with market crash. In Indian context, hence, there is immense scope for the investors to use this piece of information to design profitable trading strategyin BSE.

Apart from the presence of a special trend in the market, BSE is characterized by the presence of significant volatility in stock return. The volatility responds asymmetrically toward good and bad news with sharper reaction toward bad news. The asymmetric responses (the 'leverage' effect) tend to be sharper during the pre-crisis period rather than in the post-crisis period. The 'normal' positive relationship between risk and return seems to exist in the market. However, the correlation coefficient between risk and return starts declining and becomes negative (or even zero) as the market dips into crisis. Distinct and persistent trends thus are perceptible in the Indian stock market leaving the efficient market hypothesis on trial. Such trends could skillfully be used by investors to design profit making strategies to beat the market.

Let us now consider the other stock exchange, namely the NSE and explore whether the movements and other characteristics in the NSE resemble the trends in BSE. While exploring the issues, we shall be following the same methodologies that were followed in the previous sections. Hence, we are not repeating the methodology, but reporting the results only focusing on the analytical discussion.

2.6 Trends and Latent Structure in Indian Stock Market: National Stock Exchange

1. *Trends over the entire period: 2005 January to 2012 September*

The analysis of market movement in NSE starts from the analysis of correlation among the different indexes. Table 2.10 reveals significant correlation pattern in the NSE.

While statistically significant correlation exists among the sectoral returns, correlation between the market and the sectoral returns has been almost negligible. This is in sharp contrast with the trends in BSE. While in BSE all the sectors and the market were intertwined, NSE market is likely to be segregated from the sectors as a whole. Such a simple correlation analysis, however, hardly suffices to establish such segregation. EFA might help us better analyze the trends.

The KMO measure of sampling adequacy takes a value of 0.89 and Bartlett's test statistic of sphericity is significant at one percent level of significance implying validity of using EFA on our data set.

On the basis of eigenvalue, two factors are extracted. The first factor with an eigenvalue of 9.129, explains 70 % of total variability. The second factor has an eigenvalue of 1.006 and explains 8 % of total variability. The first factor contains all the sectoral indexes that are highly loaded in that factor. The Cronbach's alpha stands at 0.95 and declines with exclusion of each index. This makes the extracted structure a valid one. The second factor contains the market index only (Table 2.11).

Identification of two factors reveals presence of two structures, and hence two dominant trends in the NSE. All the sectors move in similar fashion and direction (as reflected in their positive loadings on the factor) and together they constitute the broad, dominant trend in NSE. The sectoral returns however are completely dissociated from the market trend. The sectoral trend happens to be more dominant than the market itself. The detailed analysis of such broad, dominant trend could be of further interest.

Analysis of market trend in NSE: use of factor score

The use of EFA on our data set for NSE extracts two factors that could be thought of as representing the broad trends in the stock market. Now we construct

34

2 Trends in Indian Stock Market: Scope for Designing Profitable Trading Rule?

Table 2.10 Correlation matrix among NSE index returns (2005–2012)

	Como	Energy	Finance	FMCG	Infra	IT	Metal	MNC	Pharma	PSE	PSU Bank	Service
ENERGY	0.93											
FINANCE	0.82	0.79										
FMCG	0.69	0.65	0.63									
INFRA	0.90	0.87	0.84	0.67								
IT	0.67	0.65	0.65	0.55	0.66							
METAL	0.89	0.76	0.73	0.61	0.79	0.61						
MNC	0.86	0.80	0.78	0.79	0.85	0.67	0.77					
PHARMA	0.71	0.66	0.63	0.63	0.69	0.59	0.61	0.72				
PSE	0.93	0.92	0.79	0.66	0.88	0.62	0.78	0.81	0.68			
PSUBANK	0.67	0.63	0.79	0.51	0.68	0.47	0.59	0.63	0.50	0.66		
SERVICE	0.89	0.87	0.93	0.68	0.93	0.82	0.78	0.83	0.70	0.86	0.72	
MARKET	0.10	0.10	0.13	0.05	0.09	0.10	0.10	0.08	0.03	0.09	0.11	0.13

2.6 Trends and Latent Structure in Indian Stock Market: National Stock Exchange

Table 2.11 Factor loadings in the factors extracted: entire period

Sectors	1	2
Commodity	0.958	–
Energy	0.916	–
Finance	0.893	–
FMCG	0.772	–
Infrastructure	0.939	–
IT	0.756	–
Market	–	0.986
Metal	0.855	–
MNC	0.913	–
Pharmaceutical	0.779	–
PSE	0.922	–
PSUBank	0.741	–
Service	0.954	–

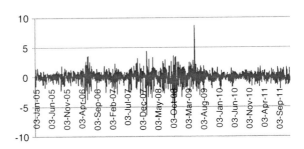

Fig. 2.15 Movements in factor scores for factor 1(NSE sector) (2005–2012)

factor scores for the two uncorrelated factors. These factor scores, just like our earlier analysis, would serve as a proxy for the latent structure of the market and help us analyze the stock market trend in proper or effective way.

The factor scores for the first factor would depict the movement or behavior at the sectoral level. Such trends will henceforth be described as the *sectoral trend*. The sectoral trend is depicted in Fig. 2.15. As is evident from the diagram, the sectoral return movement is highly volatile, characterized by the presence of volatility clustering where periods of high (low) volatility are followed by periods of high (low) volatility. The period of financial crisis that is the period of 2007–2009 is characterized by high volatility.

The factor scores for the second factor reflects the movement in NSE market index and would be henceforth described as reflecting the *market trend*. The market trend is depicted in Fig. 2.16. Just like the trends at the sectoral level, the market movements volatile are characterized by the presence of volatility clustering where periods of high (low) volatility are followed by periods of high (low) volatility. The period of financial crisis that is the period of 2007–2009 is characterized by high volatility.

However, from the simple plot it is difficult to form any proper or conclusive idea regarding the trends and nature of movements.

Fig. 2.16 Movements in factor scores for factor 2 (NSE market) (2005–2012)

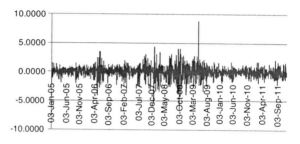

Fig. 2.17 Cycle in the sectoral return (NSE) (2005–2012)

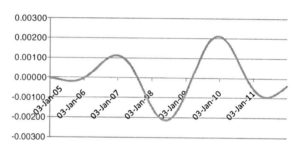

Just like our earlier analysis, trends at market and sectoral levels would now be analyzed by bringing out the nature of the cycle inherent in the series. Toward the purpose, the study uses once again the method of band pass (frequency) filter. Both the series are found to be level stationary using Augmented Dickey Fuller test statistic (null hypothesis of unit root is rejected at one percent level of significance). We chose to de-trend the data before filtering. The cycle for the sectoral return is depicted in Fig. 2.17.

The cycle for the sectoral return enables us to identify the ups and downs in NSE sectoral indexes. The *sectors* as a whole experience a boom during the phases namely, 2006–2007, 2009–2010, and since early 2012. The trends are similar to those experienced in the context of BSE. The *sectors* as a whole slide down from its peak over the periods namely, 2007–2008 and 2010–2011. Our analysis is concentrated around the first cycle. This cycle, however, is in terms of return in the sectors.

The market return cycle is depicted in Fig. 2.18. The nature of the cycle is exactly similar to those experienced at the sectoral level.

Fig. 2.18 Cycle in the market return (NSE) (2005–2012)

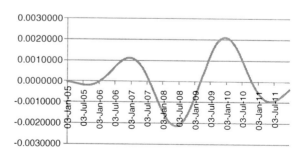

2.6 Trends and Latent Structure in Indian Stock Market: National Stock Exchange

Although the two latent structures in the market are uncorrelated, the cycles are similar at the sectoral as well as at the market level. States of economy (recovery or recession) are having similar impacts on sectoral and market level.

The trend is further analyzed through an examination of the risk-return relationship in the market as a whole. The variance of a series could serve as a good proxy for the risk of the series. As is suggested by the simple plot of the *market* and *sectoral* return, the two series are characterized by volatility clustering or volatility pooling. Moreover, the two series are negatively skew, highly peaked, and non-normal. Such series are best analyzed by an appropriate GARCH family model and risk for such a series is proxied best by its conditional variance.

The two series are modeled best by simple GARCH model of order (1, 1). The two series are hence not characterized by asymmetric response of volatility toward positive and negative announcements in the market. There is no evidence that the market or the sectors reacts more toward the negative news than toward the good news. The sectoral return as a whole is characterized by significant presence of ARCH (or, the news) effect and GARCH (the own past volatility) impacts. The ARCH effect (0.12), however, is weaker than the GARCH effect (0.87). Hence, past volatility, rather than past news at the sectoral level has relatively stronger impact on present volatility of the sectoral return. The market return is also characterized by significant presence of ARCH (0.11) and GARCH (0.88) effects with GARCH effects stronger than the ARCH effects. The results are similar to those obtained for the sectoral level. The ARCH effect at the sectoral level is marginally higher and GARCH effect is marginally lower compared to the market level.

The conditional volatility for the sectoral return is saved and depicted in Fig. 2.19.

The conditional variance, after de-trending, exhibits significant cyclical pattern (Fig. 2.20).

The conditional volatility has been significantly higher during the period of financial crisis of 2007–2008. The two other peaks are not at all significant compared to this peak. The trend reminds us about the trend in BSE over the same period. Once again, the nature of cycle of conditional variance is completely opposite to the cyclical nature of the return series. Return peaks are always associated with low conditional variance or conditional variance slumps. This is further analyzed and

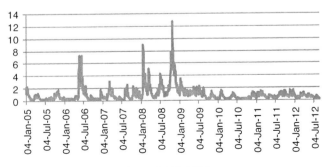

Fig. 2.19 NSE sectoral conditional variance (2005–2012)

Fig. 2.20 Cycle in the NSE sectoral conditional variance (2005–2012)

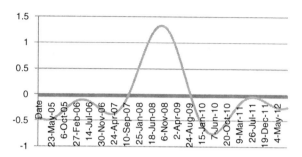

depicted in Fig. 2.21. The nature of time-varying conditional correlation between sectoral return in NSE and conditional variance is used to bring out the relationship between risk and return at the sectoral level in NSE. Like the previous section, the conditional correlation has been computed using a multivariate GARCH technique that models the variance–covariance matrix of a financial time series. A multivariate GARCH of appropriate order has been estimated for the data on two factor scores for NSE return and NSE conditional variance and the conditional correlation values have been saved. The movement in this conditional correlation reflects the risk-return relationship in the context of NSE.

The risk-return relationship has been negative and falling until mid-2006. During the period that immediately preceded the crisis, risk-return relationship started rising. However, it remained negative until mid 2007. As crisis set in, the risk-return relationship became positive and continued to rise. As crisis continued, risk-return relationship at the NSE sectoral level remained constant and positive. However, as the economy was recovering, the conditional correlation between risk and return started dwindling. Eventually, the risk-return relationship became negative.

Let us now consider the conditional variance at the market level. The market is highly volatile and the volatility has been significantly higher during the period of financial crisis. The trend could be better analyzed if we could consider the cycle in volatility at the market level (Fig. 2.22).

The cycle in market return volatility in NSE is depicted in Fig. 2.23. The nature of the cycle is similar, however not identical, to that in the sectoral return. Volatility remained constant at a very high level during the period of financial crisis. Volatility has been much lower during the pre-crisis and the post-crisis periods.

Fig. 2.21 Cycle of risk-return relationship at NSE sectoral level (2005–2012)

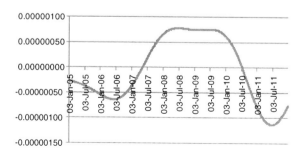

2.6 Trends and Latent Structure in Indian Stock Market: National Stock Exchange

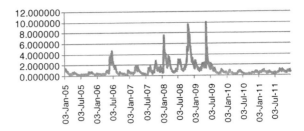

Fig. 2.22 NSE market conditional variance (2005–2012)

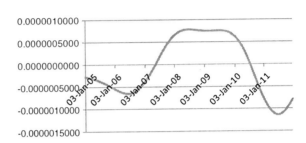

Fig. 2.23 Cycle in the NSE market conditional variance (2005–2012)

However, volatility started mounting as the market was approaching the crisis. As the market was recovering volatility dwindled to reach the floor.

The risk-return relationship at the market level, however, has been different at the market level rather than at the sectoral level in NSE. Risk-return relationship has been negative during the period of January 2005 to January 2007. However, as the economy was approaching the crisis since mid-2006, the correlation between risk and return started rising. As the economy was plunging into crisis, the correlation fluctuated but remained negative. The correlation became positive only in the post-crisis period and eventually started dwindling since mid-2010 (Fig. 2.24).

The analysis of overall market trend would now be supplemented by analyses of market trend before and after the crisis.

2. *The trends in NSE in the pre-crisis period: 2005 January to 2008 January*

The analysis of trends in the market in the pre-crisis period starts from identification of latent structure in the market.

Table 2.12 suggests presence of statistically significant correlation among different sectoral returns. The market returns however are not strongly correlated

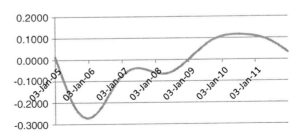

Fig. 2.24 Cycle of risk-return relationship at NSE market level (2005–2012)

Table 2.12 Correlation matrix among NSE index returns (2005–2008)

	Como	Energy	Finance	FMCG	Infra	IT	Metal	MNC	Pharma	PSE	PSU bank	Service
ENERGY	0.94											
FINANCE	0.79	0.76										
FMCG	0.75	0.71	0.65									
INFRA	0.91	0.87	0.81	0.72								
IT	0.67	0.64	0.64	0.57	0.67							
METAL	0.85	0.71	0.67	0.65	0.76	0.60						
MNC	0.87	0.80	0.76	0.84	0.86	0.67	0.75					
PHARMA	0.76	0.71	0.67	0.68	0.74	0.61	0.65	0.76				
PSE	0.95	0.96	0.77	0.71	0.88	0.65	0.77	0.82	0.73			
PSUBANK	0.75	0.70	0.91	0.59	0.75	0.55	0.63	0.70	0.63	0.71		
SERVICE	0.88	0.86	0.90	0.70	0.92	0.84	0.74	0.83	0.74	0.86	0.82	
MARKET	0.18	0.17	0.24	0.11	0.18	0.18	0.14	0.15	0.09	0.17	0.22	0.24

with the sectoral returns. The results are same as those obtained for the entire period.

The use of EFA over the pre-crisis data set is further justified by the favorable values of the KMO measure of sampling adequacy and Bartlett's tests for data adequacy. The KMO measure of sampling adequacy takes a value of 0.897 and Bartlett's test statistic of sphericity is significant at one percent level of significance implying validity of using EFA on the pre-crisis data set.

On the basis of eigenvalue two factors are retained that are uncorrelated with one another. This signifies the presence of two dominant but distinct trends in the NSE during the pre-crisis period. The first factor with an eigenvalue of 9.373 could explain 72 % of total variability. All the sectoral indexes have strong and positive loading in the first factor. The Cronbach's alpha stands at 0.9750 (which is higher than the *entire period*) and declines with exclusion of each index. This makes the extracted structure a valid one. Thus the sectors are strongly connected, move in similar fashion and direction and together they constitute the dominant trend in the market in the pre-crisis period.The second factor has the market index with strong loading in it. The market thus is completely decoupled from the sectors that are closely connected among themselves. The second factor with an eigenvalue of 1.01 could explain only 7.76 % of total variability in the NSE (Table 2.13).

The detailed analysis of such broad, dominant trend in the *pre-crisis* period would be our further area of analysis.

Analysis of market trend in NSE in pre-crisis period: use of factor score

Factor scores are constructed for the two factors extracted for the NSE. The factor scores for the first factor represent the sectoral behavior in the market. The market movement will be proxied by the second factor score. The movement or behavior of sectoral returns as a whole (given by the factor scores), henceforth described as the *sectors in pre-crisis period*, is depicted in Fig. 2.25. As is evident from the diagrams, the market as well as sectoral movements are highly volatile, characterized by the presence of volatility clustering where periods of high (low)

Table 2.13 Factor loadings in the factors extracted: pre-crisis period (NSE)

	Factor 1	Factor 2
Commodity	0.958	–
Energy	0.915	–
Finance	0.853	–
FMCG	0.819	–
Infrastructure	0.933	–
IT	0.747	–
Market	–	0.966
Metal	0.833	–
MNC	0.919	–
Pharmaceutical	0.83	–
PSE	0.929	–
PSUBANK	0.797	–
Service	0.933	–

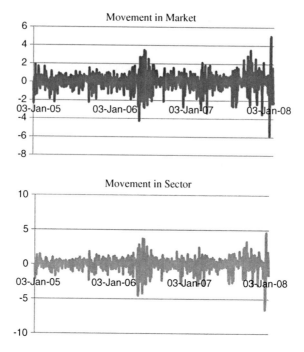

Fig. 2.25 Movements in factor scores, NSE (2005–2008)

volatility are followed by periods of high (low) volatility. However, from the simple plots it is difficult to form any idea regarding the trends and nature of movements properly. The trend in the *pre-crisis period* resembles that for the *entire Period*.

The trend could be better analyzed if it is possible to bring out the nature of the cycle inherent in the series. The cycle in the *pre-crisis* sectoral and market movements are depicted in Fig. 2.26. The cycles are generated once again using the method of band pass (frequency) filter in its CF form. Both the *pre-crisis* series

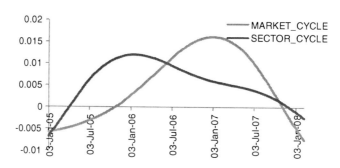

Fig. 2.26 Cycles in the NSE return (2005–2008)

2.6 Trends and Latent Structure in Indian Stock Market: National Stock Exchange

are found to be level stationary using Augmented Dickey Fuller test statistic (null hypothesis of unit root is rejected at one percent level of significance). We chose to de-trend the data before filtering. The sectoral return reached top during January 2006 and falls then after. The market, however, reached peak in January 2007 and then plummeted. As the market was riding high, the sectors were offering higher returns than the market ("beating the market", perhaps). During the recession, sectoral returns remained considerably lower than the market return. The sectoral peak, however, has been lower than the market peak.

The trend is further analyzed through examination of the risk-return relationship in the market as a whole. The variance of a series could serve as a good proxy for the risk of the series. As is suggested by the simple plots of the market and sectoral returns, the series are characterized by volatility clustering or volatility pooling. Moreover, the series are negatively skew, highly peaked, and non-normal. Such series are best analyzed by an appropriate GARCH family model and risk for such a series are proxied best by their conditional variance.

The NSE return is modeled best by simple GARCH model of order (1, 1). The market, as well as sectors as a whole is characterized by significant ARCH and GARCH effects. The ARCH coefficients are 0.21 and 0.26 respectively for the market and the sector. The GARCH coefficients for the market and sectors as a whole are 0.71 and 0.67 respectively. Thus past volatility impacts on present volatility are stronger than the news impact for the market as well as sectors. Past volatility impacts however are relatively stronger and news impacts are relatively weaker for the market rather than the sectors. This is in line with the results obtained for the entire period. The conditional volatilities for the *pre-crisis* series are saved and depicted in Fig. 2.27.

The conditional variance, after de-trending, exhibits significant cyclical pattern. Both the cycles in the conditional variance have been of inverted u shape. Volatility increased, reached a top and then fell for both the sector and the market. When market volatility was rising, sectoral volatility was higher than the market volatility up to a certain point. The sectoral volatility reached its peak much before the crisis had set in and much before the market volatility did so. The conditional volatility in market increased significantly and remained high as the economy was approaching the crisis. The diagram shows a comparative study of risks (given by

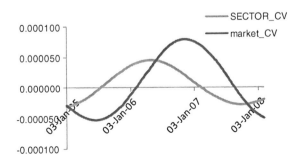

Fig. 2.27 Cycle in the factor score conditional variance (NSE: 2005–2008)

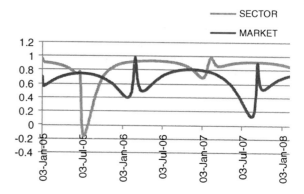

Fig. 2.28 Return-risk relationship NSE (2005–2008)

the conditional variance) at the sectoral and the market level. The risk-return relationship in the NSE is further analyzed and depicted in Fig. 2.28.

The nature of time-varying conditional correlation brings out the presence of a positive relationship between risk and return in the NSE as a whole. While the correlation fluctuates, it started declining sharply since early-2007 for the market and plummeted to a very low level in mid-2007. The risk-return correlation in the market was increasing sharply during the recession. The sectoral correlation has mostly been higher than the correlation at the market level. The sectoral correlation dropped to a low level only during mid-2005. The financial crisis of 2007–2008 did not have much impact on the risk-return correlation at the sectoral level. For most of the times, the value of correlation coefficient remained higher than 0.8.

3. *The trends in the post-crisis period: 2008 February to 2012 September*

The analysis of market trend in the post-crisis period starts from identification of latent structure in the market.

Table 2.14 suggests presence of statistically significant correlation among sectoral returns during the post-crisis period. The correlation between the market and the sector, however, has been quite low and in significant. The results are similar to those obtained for the previous phases. The correlation coefficients are more or less the same in magnitude compared to those for the *entire* and *pre-crisis* period.

The use of EFA over the post-crisis period data set is once again justified by the favorable values of the KMO measure of sampling adequacy and Bartlett's tests for data adequacy. The KMO measure of sampling adequacy takes a value of 0.875 and Bartlett's test statistic of sphericity is significant at one percent level of significance implying validity of using EFA on the post-crisis data set.

On the basis of eigenvalue, once again, two factors are extracted that are uncorrelated to each other. The first factor with an eigenvalue 9.007 explains 69.29 % of total variability. The second factor with eigenvalue of 1.009 explains 7.76 % of total variability. Both the eigenvalue and the total variability explained by the single factor extracted are lower than those obtained for the *entire period* as

2.6 Trends and Latent Structure in Indian Stock Market: National Stock Exchange

Table 2.14 Correlation matrix among NSE index returns (2008–2012)

	Energy	Finance	FMCG	Infra	IT	Metal	MNC	Pharma	PSE	Psubank	Service	Market
Como	0.930	0.843	0.632	0.902	0.673	0.924	0.851	0.672	0.922	0.608	0.890	0.039
Energy	1.000	0.802	0.601	0.864	0.661	0.790	0.792	0.638	0.901	0.575	0.867	0.047
Finance	0.802	1.000	.637	0.863	0.673	0.777	0.800	0.617	0.817	0.719	0.939	0.069
FMCG	0.601	0.637	1.000	0.635	0.562	0.569	0.748	0.582	0.602	0.437	0.667	0.010
Infra	0.864	0.863	0.635	1.000	0.662	0.814	0.846	0.666	0.883	0.626	0.930	0.031
IT	0.661	0.673	0.562	0.662	1.000	0.622	0.675	0.578	0.611	0.434	0.819	0.057
Metal	0.790	0.777	0.569	0.814	0.622	1.000	0.788	0.583	0.782	0.551	0.808	0.065
MNC	0.792	0.800	0.748	0.846	0.675	0.788	1.000	0.687	0.796	0.582	0.838	0.035
Pharma	0.638	0.617	0.582	0.666	0.578	0.583	0.687	1.000	0.638	0.417	0.680	−0.013
PSE	0.901	0.817	0.602	0.883	0.611	0.782	0.796	0.638	1.000	0.611	0.858	0.023
Psubank	0.575	0.719	0.437	0.626	0.434	0.551	0.582	0.417	0.611	1.000	0.652	0.039
Service	0.867	0.939	0.667	0.930	0.819	0.808	0.838	0.680	0.858	0.652	1.000	0.061
Market	0.047	0.069	0.010	0.031	0.057	0.065	0.035	−0.013	0.023	0.039	0.061	1.000

Table 2.15 Factor loadings in the factors extracted (NSE): post-crisis period

	Factor 1	Factor 2
Commodity	0.957	–
Energy	0.916	–
Finance	0.919	–
FMCG	0.734	–
Infrastructure	0.942	–
IT	0.767	–
Market	–	0.992
Metal	0.876	–
MNC	0.909	–
Pharmaceutical	0.744	–
PSE	0.916	–
PSUBANK	0.690	–
Service	0.964	–

well as for the *pre-crisis* period. Once again, the first factor contains all the sectoral indexes that are highly and positively loaded in that factor. The Cronbach's alpha stands at 0.9525 (which is lower than those obtained for the *entire period* as well as for the *pre-crisis period*) and declines with exclusion of each index. This makes the extracted structure, once again a valid one. The second factor has the market index with strong loading in it (Table 2.15).

The NSE is characterized by two distinct trends in the post-crisis period. The sectors constitute the broad, dominant trend and they, among themselves are strongly correlated and move in similar fashion and similar direction even in the *post-crisis* period. All the sectors and the market move in similar fashion and direction (as reflected in their positive loadings on the factor). The detailed analysis of the dominant trends in the *post-crisis* period would be our further area of analysis.

Analysis of market trend in post-crisis period: use of factor score

Just like the previous cases, we have constructed the factor scores for the two extracted factors for the *post-crisis* period. These factor scores would serve as a proxy for the latent structure of the *post-crisis* market.

The movement or behavior of market and sectoral trends (given by the factor scores), are depicted in Fig. 2.29. As is evident from the diagram, the market and sectoral movements are highly volatile, characterized by the presence of volatility clustering where periods of high (low) volatility are followed by periods of high (low) volatility. However, from the simple plot it is difficult to form any idea regarding the trends and nature of movements properly. The trend in the *post-crisis period* resembles those for the *entire* as well as the *pre-crisis periods*. The volatility is significantly higher during the period of February 2008 to March 2009: the period when stock market was sliding.

The trend could be better analyzed if it is possible to bring out the nature of the cycle inherent in the series. The cycles are generated once again using the same method of band pass (frequency) filter in its CF form. The *post-crisis* series are

2.6 Trends and Latent Structure in Indian Stock Market: National Stock Exchange

Fig. 2.29 Movements in factor scores, NSE (2008–2012)

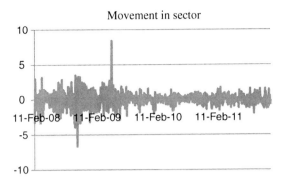

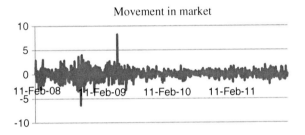

Fig. 2.30 Cycles in the sectoral and market return (NSE) (2008–2012)

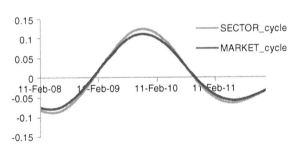

found to be level stationary using Augmented Dickey Fuller test statistic (null hypothesis of unit root is rejected at one percent level of significance). We chose to de-trend the data before filtering. The cycles are depicted in Fig. 2.30.

The cycle for the stock market enables us to identify the ups and downs in returns in the NSE in the *post-crisis* period. The sectoral and market cycles are almost similar in nature. Both the cycles are inverted u-shaped. When the economy was recovering after the crisis, sectoral returns were marginally lower than the market return. Similar behavior was observed when economy is sliding down in recent years. The sectoral peak, however, is higher than the market peak. This relationship is completely different from that obtained for the pre-crisis period.

The trend in NSE is further analyzed through examination of the risk-return relationship at the market as well as sectoral level in the *post-crisis* period. As is suggested by the simple plot of the *stock market* returns, both the series are characterized by volatility clustering or volatility pooling. Moreover the series are

Table 2.16 Application of EGARCH model on first factor score for NSE (2008-2012)

Dependent Variable: SECTOR

Method: ML—ARCH (Marquardt)—Normal distribution

Included observations: 959 after adjustments

Convergence achieved after 33 iterations

Presample variance: backcast (parameter = 0.7)

$\text{LOG(GARCH)} = C(2) + C(3)*\text{ABS(RESID}(-1)/@\text{SQRT(GARCH}(-1))) + C(4) *\text{RESID}(-1)/@\text{SQRT(GARCH}(-1)) + C(5)*\text{LOG(GARCH}(-1))$

	Variance equation			
	Coefficient	Std. error	z-statistic	Prob.
C(1)	0.006771	0.021494	0.315034	0.7527
C(2)	−0.154017	0.021982	−7.006553	0.0000
C(3)	0.189606	0.026871	7.056247	0.0000
C(4)	−0.072713	0.015861	−4.584505	0.0000
C(5)	0.986357	0.004444	221.9540	0.0000
R-squared	−0.000046	Mean dependent var		−3.13E-08
Adjusted R-squared	−0.004239	S.D. dependent var		1.000000
S.E. of regression	1.002117	Akaike info criterion		2.432335
Sum squared resid	958.0441	Schwarz criterion		2.457704
Log likelihood	−1161.304	Hannan-Quinn criter.		2.441996
Durbin–Watson stat	1.922791			

negatively skew, highly peaked, and non-normal. Such series could be best analyzed by an appropriate GARCH family model and risks for such series are proxied best by the conditional variance.

The market is modeled best by EGARCH, an asymmetric GARCH model of order (1, 1). As is suggested by Table 2.16, the sectoral return in the *post-crisis* period is characterized by asymmetric response of volatility toward positive and negative announcements in the market. The sectoral return reacts more toward the negative news than toward the good news.

The market in the *post-crisis* period is also characterized by asymmetric response of volatility toward positive and negative announcements in the market. The market reacts more toward the negative news than toward the good news (Table 2.17).

This result is in sharp contrast to what we obtained for the pre-crisis period.The conditional volatility cycles for the *post-crisis* series are depicted in Fig. 2.31.

The conditional variance, after de-trending, exhibits significant cyclical pattern. The conditional volatility has been significantly higher during the period of 2008–2009. The conditional volatility was significantly lower during late 2009–2011. Thus, volatility and hence risk, remained significantly higher during the period of crisis. The risk cycles have been almost similar in nature for the market and the sectors as a whole. As risks were falling sectoral risks were

2.6 Trends and Latent Structure in Indian Stock Market: National Stock Exchange

Table 2.17 Application of EGARCH model on second factor score for NSE (2008–2012)

Dependent Variable: MARKET
Method: ML—ARCH (Marquardt)—Normal distribution
Included observations: 959 after adjustments
Convergence achieved after 43 iterations
Presample variance: backcast (parameter = 0.7)
LOG(GARCH) = C(2) + C(3)*ABS(RESID(−1)/@SQRT(GARCH(−1))) + C(4) *RESID(−1)/@SQRT(GARCH(−1)) + C(5)*LOG(GARCH(−1))

	Variance equation			
	Coefficient	Std. Error	z-Statistic	Prob.
C(1)	0.004767	0.022068	0.216029	0.8290
C(2)	−0.144538	0.023330	−6.195442	0.0000
C(3)	0.179236	0.028700	6.245237	0.0000
C(4)	−0.059043	0.013842	−4.265462	0.0000
C(5)	0.990431	0.004079	242.7968	0.0000
R-squared	−0.000023	Mean dependent var		−6.26E-08
Adjusted R-squared	−0.004216	S.D. dependent var		1.000000
S.E. of regression	1.002106	Akaike info criterion		2.461329
Sum squared resid	958.0219	Schwarz criterion		2.486699
Log likelihood	−1175.207	Hannan-Quinn criter.		2.470991
Durbin–Watson stat	1.922218			

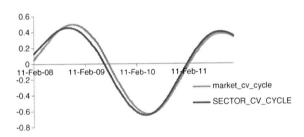

Fig. 2.31 Cycle in the NSE conditional variance (2008–2012)

marginally higher than the market risk. However, during any downfall in the market when risks were mounting sectoral risks almost coincide with the market risk.

The risk-return relationship in the NSE in the *post-crisis* period is further analyzed and depicted in Fig. 2.32. The nature of time-varying conditional correlation brings out the nature of risk-return relationship in the market. The correlation between risk and return in the market level fell just after the crisis and remained marginally positive over the entire *post-crisis* period. Risk-return relationship has been fluctuating and mostly negative at the sectoral level. The correlation became close to zero during the period of 2008–2009 when the economy was plummeted in crisis.

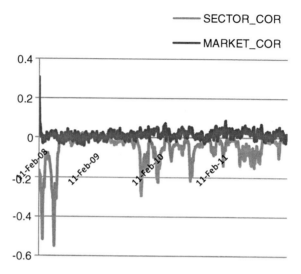

Fig. 2.32 Return-risk relationship BSE (2008–2012)

The trends in National Stock Exchange: Any 'Signal' to frame profitable trading strategy?

NSE has been dominated by two dominant trends in the market. The most dominant or 'market' trend is formed by all the sectors in the NSE. The sectors as a whole are completely decoupled from the market. The trend has lasted for the past 8 years. The sectors among themselves however are closely connected among themselves and move in similar fashion and in similar direction. Such dissociation between sectoral indexes and market index, that is independent of the states of the economy, might offer investors profitable business opportunities. Moreover, the trend in the post-crisis period is weaker than the 'average' (the trend for the entire period) market trend where as the trend in the pre-crisis period is stronger than the 'average'. This is revealed by the EFA where the single factor extracted could account for more variability (as given by the values of the eigenvectors) in the pre-

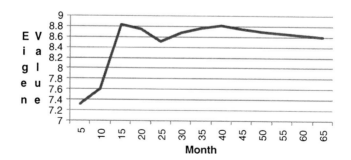

Fig. 2.33 Nature of eigenvalue for first factor in NSE (2005–2012)

crisis period than for the post-crisis period. In our earlier analysis of eigenvalue and eigenvector composition for BSE has revealed how that might provide us with significant signals that might be useful as an indicator of future events. The changing nature of eigenvalue for the first factor in NSE has been shown in Fig. 2.33. The eigenvalue has changed from month to month. The fraction of market variation captured by the first eigenvector thus changes over time. The movements are sometime marked by sharp changes.

Thus, just like BSE, when the market experiences or passes through some 'extra-ordinary' events, some 'unique' or 'special' trend persists in the market. As the economy reverts back to its 'normal' state this 'special' trend weakens in the sense that the variability captured by the first factor declines steadily. For investors this information might be extremely useful in designing profitable trading strategy. To be more specific, if it is possible to identify when this special trend would set in or how long it would last, investors might be able to design strategies to make profit out of market movements. The movements in the first factor eigenvalue reveal few more observations. The eigenvalue increases during the periods of recovery and reaches maximum just before the peak. During a stable period, however, the eigenvalue falls or reaches a plateau. Therefore, the 'special' trend persists during the phases of recovery and weakens during the periods of recession or stability. The market crash could be predicted from a high eigenvalue of the first factor and high eigenvalue could be associated with market crash. In the Indian context, hence, there is immense scope for investors to use this piece of information to design a profitable trading strategy in the National Stock Exchange.

While it is evident that some trading or fruitful investment strategies could be derived for the Indian stock market, it would be of interest to explore how such strategies could be framed. That is where we move to next.

References

Abraham B, Wei W (1984) Inferences about the parameters of a time series model with changing variance. Metrika 31(1):183–194

Aggarwal R, Inclan C, Leal R (1999) Volatility in emerging stock markets. J Finan Quant Anal 34:33–55

Altissimo F, Corradi V (2003) Strong rules for detecting the number of breaks in a time series. J Econometrics 117(2):207–244

Andrews DWK (1993) Tests for parameter instability and structural change with unknown change point. Econometrica 61:821–856

Andrews DWK, Ploberger W (1994) Optimal tests when a nuisance parameter is present only under the alternative. Econometrica 62:1383–1414

Baba Y, Engle RF, Kraft D, Kroner K (1990) Multivariate simultaneous generalized ARCH. University of California, San Diego (Unpublished manuscript)

Bai J (1994) Least squares estimation of a shift in linear processes. J Time Ser Anal 15:453–472

Bai J (1997) Estimation of a change point in multiple regression models. Rev Econ Statist 79:551–563

Bai J, Perron P (2003) Computation and analysis of multiple structural change models. J Appl Econom 18(1):1–22

Banerjee A, Lumsdaine RL, Stock JH (1992) Recursive and sequential tests of the unit root and trend break hypotheses: theory and international evidence. J Bus Econ Statist 10:271–287

Baufays P, Rasson JP (1985) Variance changes in autoregressive models. In: Anderson OD (ed) Time series analysis: theory and practice, 7th edn. North Holland, New York

Bollerslev T, Engle RF, Wooldridge JM (1988) A capital asset pricing model with time varying covariances. J Pol Econ 96(1):116–131

Brooks C, Henry OT (2000) Linear and non-linear transmission of equity return volatility: evidence from the US, Japan and Australia. Econ Model 17:497–513

Cheng T (2009) An efficient algorithm for estimating a change-point. Stat Probabil Lett 79:559–565

Chu CSJ, White H (1992) A direct test for changing trend. J Bus Econ Statist 10:189–199

Gonzalo J, Pitarakis JY (2002) Estimation and model selection based inference in single and multiple threshold models. J Econometrics 110:319–352

Gregory AW, Hansen BE (1996) Residual-based tests for cointegration in the models with regime shifts. J Econometrics 70:99–126

Hair JF, Black WC, Babin BJ, Anderson R (2010) Multivariate data analysis, 7th edn. Pearson Education Inc, India

Hansen BE (1990) Lagrange multiplier tests for parameter instability in non-linear models. Unpublished manuscript, University of Rochester, Rochester, New York. http://www.ssc.wisc.edu/~bhansen/paper/LMTests.pdf. Accessed 21 Sept 2010

Hansen BE (1992) Test for Instability with I(1) processes. J Bus Econ Statist 10:321–335

Hansen BE (2001) The new econometrics of structural change: dating breaks in U.S. labor productivity. J Econ Perspect 15(4):117–128

Hsu A, Miller RB, Wichern DW (1974) On the stable Paretian behavior of stock-market prices. J Am Statistical Assoc 69(345):108–113

Huang B, Yang C (2001) The impact of settlement time on the volatility of stock market revisited: an application of the iterated cumulative sums of squares detection method for changes of variance. Appl Econ Lett 8:665–668

Inclan C, Tiao GC (1994) Use of cumulative sums of squares for retrospective detection of changes of variance. J Am Statistical Assoc 89:913–923

Ismail MT, Isa Z (2006) Modelling exchange rates using regime switching models. Sains Malaysiana 35(2):55–62

Karunanayake I, Valadkhani A, O'Brien M (2008) Modelling Australian stock market volatility: a multivariate GARCH approach. Economics Working Paper series, University of Wollongong, http://www.uow.edu.au/commerce/econ/wpapers.html, Accessed on 12 Aug 2010

Lumsdaine RL, Papell DH (1997) Multiple trend breaks and the unit root hypothesis. Rev Econ Statist 79:223–230

Marcucci J (2005) Forecasting stock market volatility with regime-switching GARCH models. Stud Nonlinear 9(4). Dynam Econometrics 9(4):1–53 (Article 6)

Nelson CR, Plosser CI (1982) Trends and random walks in macroeconomic time series. J Monet Econ 10:139–162

Perron P (1989) The great crash, the oil-price shock and the unit-root hypothesis. Econometrica 57:1361–1401

Perron P (1990) Testing for a unit root in a time series with a changing mean. J Bus Econ Statist 8:153–162

Perron P (1997a) Further evidence on breaking trend functions in macroeconomic variables. J Econometrics 80(2):355–385

Perron P (1997b) L'estimation de Modèles avec Changements Structurels Multiples. L'Actual Econ 73(1):457–505

Perron P, Vogelsang TJ (1992) Nonstationarity and level shifts with an application to purchasing power parity. J Bus Econ Statist 10:301–320

References

Sansó A, Aragó V, Carrion-i-Silvestre JL1 (2004) Testing for Changes in the Unconditional Variance of Financial Time Series. Revista Econ Financiera 4:32–53

Schaller H, Norden SV (1997) Regime switching in stock market returns. Appl Finan Econ 7(2):177–191

Scherrer W, Ribarits E (2007) On the parameterization of multivariate GARCH models. Econometric Theory 23:464–484

Tsay RS (1988) Outliers, level shifts and variance changes in time series. J Forecast 7:1–20

Valentinyi-Endrész M (2004) Structural breaks and financial risk management. MNB Working Papers 2004/11, Magyar Nemzeti Bank, The Central Bank of Hungary. http://english.mnb.hu/Root/Dokumentumtar/ENMNB/Kiadvanyok/mnben_mnbfuzetek/mnben_wp200411/wp2004_11v.pdf. Accessed 2 January 2009

Wilson B, Aggarwal R, Inclan C (1996) Detecting volatility changes across the oil sector. J Futures Markets 16:313–330

Zivot E, Andrews DWK (1992) Further evidence on the great crash, the oil price shock, and the unit-root hypothesis. J Bus Econ Statist 10:251–270

Chapter 3
Possible Investment Strategies in Indian Stock Market

Abstract This chapter explores the presence of possible and profitable investment strategies in the Indian stock market. The exploratory factor analysis used in Chap. 2 explored the presence of a distinct latent structure in the Indian stock market. Given the latent structures in the BSE and NSE, it is indeed possible for investors to design profitable investment strategies. Both risk-averse and risk-loving investors might find portfolios suitable for them based on different indicators such as return, risk-adjusted return, systematic, and unsystematic risk. The nature of such portfolios, however, has changed over time. The financial crisis of 2007–2008 has affected some sectors adversely, while some have been able to avoid the impact of the crisis. Some defensive sectors have emerged out of the crisis with an aggressive tenor. Portfolios in BSE and NSE moreover have some characteristics in common. Such discernable patterns in portfolio choice, however, will put Efficient Market Hypothesis on trial.

Keywords Investment strategy · Risk-adjusted return · Unique risk · Market risk · Portfolio construction

> *The early bird gets the worm, but the second mouse gets the cheese.*
>
> Anonymous

3.1 Introduction

The modern portfolio construction theory revolves around the fact that assets of different categories behave differently from one another. This implies that an asset from a different class has its own unique risk and return profile. They respond differently to different economic events and during cycles. The idea of combining various asset classes, each with unique attributes, is the basis for building a diversified portfolio. Any rational investor, however, will always try to build-up a portfolio with less-risky assets that provide high return: a portfolio that is very difficult, if not impossible, to construct in the real world. It is then a headache for the investors to construct a "perfect" portfolio, or a portfolio that closely resembles the "perfect" one.

Markowitz (1952) asserted that while investing in financial assets, looking at the returns and associated risks is not sufficient. By choosing and combining more than one stock, it is possible to reduce riskiness of investment: *one should not put all the eggs in one basket*. The risk in a portfolio of diverse individual stocks will be less than the risk inherent in holding any one of the individual stocks (provided the risks of the various stocks are not positively related). Effective investment, however, does not mean either picking or combining stocks at random. Rather, it is the combination of stocks that matters: *find out the right baskets to keep the eggs*.

The Modern portfolio theory suggests that the risk for individual stock returns could be decomposed into two: (1) the Systematic Risk Component or the market risks that cannot be diversified away and (2) the Unsystematic Risk or the risk specific to individual stocks that can be diversified away as one increases the number of stocks in the portfolio. For a well-diversified portfolio, individual stock risks add very little to portfolio risk. Instead, it is the correlation between individual stocks' return that determines overall portfolio risk.

The history of financial market movement, however, makes us realize that portfolio theory is just a theory in itself. At the end of the day, a portfolio's success rests on the investor's skills and the time he or she devotes to it. Sometimes it is better to pick a small number of out-of-favor investments and wait for the market to turn in your favor than to rely on market averages alone. Moreover, it is hard to beat the market. Some beat the market, no doubt, by taking up excessive risk, but they get their retribution as markets slide down.

Using the information on the latent structure of the Indian stock market let us now concentrate on some of the possible and profitable investment strategies.

3.2 Investment Strategies in BSE

The BSE is characterized by a single latent structure that includes all the sectors and the market index. The sectors and the market are closely connected among themselves. Any portfolio construction by any rational investor is based on a simple rule of thumb: the returns of the assets constituting the portfolio should not be very closely related, or even if they are strongly connected, the correlation among the stock returns should be strongly negative. As revealed by the exploratory factor analysis the possible portfolios will have to be constructed using some assets whose returns are closely connected. We shall, in our further analysis consider the possible portfolio construction over the three subphases of the study.

The construction of portfolio is based on some indicators described as follows:

Indicator of average return: The average returns are calculated for the market and the sectoral indexes.

3.2 Investment Strategies in BSE

Indicator of unique risk: A multivariate GARCH of appropriate order has been estimated taking all the sectors and the market as a 'system'. The conditional variances are saved and are used as proxy for unique risk of the Index.

Indicator of market risk: The conditional correlations obtained from the estimation of multivariate GARCH have been used as proxies for market risk. This type of risk has been once again categorized into two: the conditional correlation among the sectoral return would proxy for the cross-sectoral risk, the individual sector's risk with respect to other sectors; and the conditional correlation between a sector and the market would serve as the proxy for the market beta.

Indicator of risk-adjusted return: The Sharpe Index defined as $(R_i - R_F)/S_i$, where R_i, R_F and S_i are returns of i'th asset, risk free rate, and standard deviation of R_i respectively, serving as proxy for the risk-adjusted return.

Let us now consider some possible portfolios under these circumstances.

3.2.1 Portfolio Construction in BSE: 2005–2012

The sectors and market indexes could be arranged as shown in Table 3.1. The sectors could be categorized broadly into four groups. The bank and the consumer durable indexes earn above average return with above average unique risk. The automobile, capital goods, and FMCG sectors earn above return at below average return. The metal, PSU, and IT sectors earn below average return at above average risk. The market index too falls under this category. Healthcare, Oil and Natural Gas, and Power sectors earn low return at low risk. The market risks are in line with the unique risks. The sectors with high unique risk have very high conditional correlation among themselves and with the market.

Table 3.1 Categorization of BSE indexes: 2005–2012

Index	Return-risk	Cross-correlation	Risk-adjusted return ranking	Correlation with market
	(in comparison with respective averages)			
Bank	High return, high	HIGH	Sharpe 4	HIGH
CD	risk		Sharpe 2	
Auto	High return, low	LOW	Sharpe 3	LOW
CG	risk		Sharpe 6	
FMCG			Sharpe 1	
Metal	Low return, high	HIGH	Sharpe 12	HIGH
PSU	risk		Sharpe 11	
IT			Sharpe 10	
SENSEX	Low return, high risk	HIGH		
HC	Low return, low	LOW	Sharpe 5	LOW
ONG	risk		Sharpe 8	Moderately high
Power			Sharpe 9	Moderately high

The risk lover and risk averse: the study defines a risk lover investor as one who loves taking risk irrespective of the extent of returns earned. A risk-averse investor, on the other hand, will be interested in higher return at the cost of lower risk. Or, alternatively, they would prefer higher risk-adjusted returns. Given the scenario, the possible portfolios for the investors in the BSE might be the following:

Investment Strategy 1: A high-return, high-risk group The portfolio would consist of the BSE Bank Index and BSE Consumer Durable Index. Both the indexes earn above average returns. The BSE CD and Bank Index returns have been the second and fourth highest in the market. The portfolio would thus earn above average return. The unique risk, however, for the individual Indexes has been substantially high. For each index return, the cross-correlation and the correlation with the market have also been quite high. The risk of the portfolio thus would be very high. The risk-adjusted returns, however, are quite high for the two indexes. This might imply that an investor, not so risk-lover and interested in high risk-adjusted-return might also accept the portfolio.

Investment Strategy 2: A low-return, high-risk group The low-return-high (both unique and market)-risk portfolio will be accepted neither by the risk lover nor by the risk-averse investor. This is simply for the reason that the risk-lover would never accept below average return for taking above average risks. The low Sharpe ratios for the indexes concerned would make risk-averse investors disinterested in the portfolio. The group, however, could be combined with other groups to make profitable portfolios.

Investment Strategy 3: A combination of (1) high-return, high-risk and (2) low-return, high-risk group This portfolio, by nature, is extremely risky. The portfolio would consist of the Bank, Consumer Durable, Metal, PSU, IT, and possibly the market indexes. While the individual risks are substantially high, the cross-correlation among the sectoral returns and the correlation of the individual sectoral returns with that of the market have been above average. The portfolio might be preferred by extreme risk lovers. However, the low-return, high-risk group with very low Sharpe ratios will always be dominated by the other group of high-risk and high-return indexes. For an investor, who is not so risk loving, portfolio 3 will always be dominated by portfolio 1. The combination is not at all acceptable to a risk-averse investor.

Investment Strategy 4: A high-return, low-risk group The portfolio would consist of automobile, capital goods, and FMCG indexes. In terms of return, the indexes rank third, fourth, and first respectively. The unique risks are substantially lower, the three sectors being the lowest conditional variance sectors. The cross-correlations among sectors as well as correlations with the market have been the lowest possible. The FMCG, automobile, and capital goods rank first, third, and sixth respectively. This is the best place of investment for a risk-averse person.

3.2 Investment Strategies in BSE   59

Investment Strategy 5: A combination of high-return, low-risk, and low-return, low-risk group This group consists of the capital goods, FMCG, automobile, healthcare, oil and natural gas, and power sectors. The group is an extremely low-risk group. The cross-correlations among the sectoral returns have been very low. The correlation with market return has been the lowest for capital goods, FMCG, automobile, and the healthcare sectors. This correlation has been marginally higher for the oil and natural gas and power sectors. The sectors individually have been very low unique risk sectors. The portfolio could well be accepted by risk-averse investors. However, the low market risk and the high risk-adjusted return for the capital goods, FMCG, automobile, and healthcare sectors suggest that a portfolio could be constructed with them that would dominate any other combination in the group.

Investment Strategy 6: A low-return, low-risk group The group consists of the healthcare, power, and oil and natural gas sectors. The sectors possess very low unique risk. While the cross-correlations among sectoral returns have been almost below average, the market risks have been moderately high. The Sharpe ratios, however, have not been very high. The portfolio might be accepted by some risk-averse investors.

3.2.2 Portfolio Construction in BSE in the Pre-crisis Period: 2005–2008

During the pre-crisis period, as suggested by the exploratory factor analysis, there has been a single latent structure constituted of all the sectors and the market. Any portfolio construction would then be choosing among a closely connected set of assets. On the basis of risk-return relationship the indexes in the pre-crisis period could be categorized into three groups. The groups are shown in Table 3.2. There is, however, no low-return, high-risk group in the stock market.

The study now considers the possible portfolios that could be constructed during this period.

Investment Strategy 1: High-return, high-risk group This group earns above average return but possesses above average risk. The group consists of Metal, CD, Bank, CG, and Power indexes. The conditional cross-correlations among the sectoral returns are also high, except for that between CD and Bank index. The conditional correlation with market return has also been high except for that of CD. This group thus, could be favored by risk-lover investors. The risk-averse investor could choose only CD from the group that has very low market risk. However, the below average Sharpe Ratio for the sector might discourage extreme risk-averse persons to invest in the sector. Although, the high Sharpe ratio sectors belong to this group, they will fail to attract the risk-averse investors due to the high market risk associated with them.

Table 3.2 Portfolio construction in BSE in the pre-crisis period: 2005–2008

Sectors	Risk-return	Sharpe ratio rank	Cross-correlation among sectors	Correlation with market index
	In terms of corresponding averages			
Metal	High return	10	High *except between CD and*	High *except for CD*
CD	high risk	6	*bank*	
Bank		7		
CG		1		
Power		2		
ONG	High return low risk	3	–	High
SENSEX	High return low risk		–	–
IT	Low return	11	Low *except between*	Low *except for PSU*
PSU	low risk	9	*automobile and PSU*	
FMCG		4		
Automobile		8		
Healthcare		12		

Investment Strategy 2: Investment in single sector—ONG The Oil and Natural Gas Sector has been a high-mean, low-risk sector that ranks third in terms of Sharpe ratio. This sector, apart from the uncomfortable part that it has a high conditional correlation with the market, may be the choice of a risk-averse investor.

Investment Strategy 3: Investment in single sector, ONG combined with the market index Investment in ONG could be combined with the market index, since both are high-return, low-risk indexes. However, extremely risk-averse investors might be discouraged by the high conditional correlation between the two indexes.

Investment Strategy 4: Consideration for high return only (combination of investment in high-return, high-risk group and in high-return, low-risk group) In construction of such portfolio, ONG or market index or both could be combined with the High-Return, High-Risk Group. This will further increase the return of the portfolio. The fact that the unique risk of ONG index is low, however, does not necessarily mean that the portfolio risk will be minimized. The ONG index has high cross-correlation with the other members in the group as well as with the market. This portfolio therefore will be the choice of only risk-lover investors.

Investment Strategy 5: Consideration for low risk only (combination of investment in high-return, low-risk group and in low-return, low-risk group) This group will constitute of ONG, IT, PSU, FMCG, Automobile, and Healthcare indexes. The cross-correlations among the sectors are low, except for that between PSU and Automobile. PSU and ONG, on the other hand have high

3.2 Investment Strategies in BSE   61

correlation with market index. The group might be favored by risk-averse investors. However, some sub-groups could also be formed. Investment in two high-
Sharpe ratio indexes, namely ONG (rank 3) and FMCG (rank 4) could be profitable for relatively more risk-averse investor.

**Investment Strategy 6: Pessimist investment (investment in low-return, low-
risk group)** This group will constitute IT, PSU, FMCG, Automobile, and
Healthcare indexes. The cross-correlations among the sectors are very low, except
for that between PSU and Automobile. PSU on the other hand has high correlation
with market index. The group might be favored by excessively risk-averse
investors who have consideration for low risk only. However, in that context
exclusion of PSU from the portfolio could be more profitable for a pessimist
investor. One thing, however, is to be noted. Given the investment strategy 5,
investment strategy 6 will always be dominated and redundant.

3.2.3 Portfolio Construction in BSE in the Post-crisis Period: 2008–2012

The post-crisis period, unlike the pre-crisis period, is characterized by the presence
of four groups on the basis of risk-return information. The low-return, high-risk
group was absent in the pre-crisis period. The groups are shown in Table 3.3. The
sectors and the market constitute the single latent structure in the post-crisis BSE.
The portfolios are then to be constructed using a set of closely connected assets.
Under such circumstances, the study considers the following investment strategy.

Table 3.3 Portfolio construction in BSE in the post-crisis period: 2008–2012

Sectors	Risk-return	Sharpe ratio rank	Cross-correlation among sectors	Correlation with market index
	In terms of corresponding averages			
IT	High return high risk	5(−)	High	High
CG		11(−)		
Metal		7(−)		
HC	High return low risk	3	Low	Low
Automobile		4		
Power	Low return high risk	10(−)	High	High
ONG	*(negative return)*	9(−)		
CD		2		
Bank		6(−)		
FMCG	Low return low risk	1	Low	High
PSU	*(negative return)*	8(−)		
SENSEX	Low return low risk *(negative return)*			

Investment Strategy 1: High-return, high-risk group The group consists of the IT, CG, and Metal sectors. The sectors have high unique risk as well as high market risks. The group might be preferred by risk-loving investors only. The Negative Sharpe ratio for each of these sectoral indexes will discourage risk-averse investors to invest in this group. This is the only profitable portfolio for the risk-lovers. The point will be evidenced from the investment strategy 2.

Investment Strategy 2: Low-return, high-risk group This group consists of Power, ONG, CD, and Bank indexes. The group will hardly be chosen by any rational investors because of the negative returns offered by the sectors in the post-crisis period. Although the consumers' durable index possesses a high Sharpe ratio (rank 2), risk-averse investors are unlikely to choose the sector as a profitable place for investment because of its negative return. The group or its members, either in isolation or in combination with others, will not be chosen by the Investors. This makes the group redundant from the point of view of investment.

Investment Strategy 3: Low-return, low-risk group By the similar logic, the low-return, low-risk group will also be a redundant choice for investment. Usually these types of assets are preferred by extremely risk-averse investors. This group contains FMCG sector, the sector with the highest Sharpe ratio. Nonetheless, investors may not find the sector an attractive place of investment due to the negative returns offered by it.

Investment Strategy 4: High-return, low-risk group This group consists of the Healthcare and the Automobile sectors. This combination is a risk-averse investor's delight to invest in. Apart from the fact that the two sectors are of above average return and below average risks, they rank high (Rank 2 and 3, respectively) in terms of the Sharpe ratio. This group may be combined with the group of high-return, high-risk assets judiciously to construct a profitable portfolio.

Now, the study may proceed to compare the investment strategies in the pre- and post-crisis periods for BSE. The pre-crisis period is characterized by the presence of three groups in terms of risk-return relationship. The low-return, high-risk group does not exist in the pre-crisis period. The risk of investment thus was lower in the pre-crisis period. The risk-lover as well as risk-averse investors was able to design profitable investment strategies by judicious selection and combination of the constituents of the three groups. The post-crisis period is different in the sense that the low-return, high-risk group exists along with the three others. However, the choice of investment is much limited in the post-crisis period. This is particularly because of the low and even negative returns earned by many sectors in the post-crisis period. Hence, the groups consisted of the low (and, negative) return sectors become redundant for Investors' choice. There have been some striking similarities in the nature of the sectoral returns also. Metal and CG have always remained high-return, high-risk sectors. FMCG and PSU, on the other hand, have remained low-return, low-risk sectors. There is however, a significant difference. The FMCG and PSU were earning negative returns in the post crisis period. Thus, crisis has affected the sectors adversely in terms of return. Healthcare and automobile have remained low risk but changed their return characteristics with the cycle in the economy. From low-return sectors in the pre-crisis period, they turned out to be high-return ones in the post-crisis period. The crisis has transformed the IT sector from a defensive low-return, low-risk sector into an aggressive high-return, high-risk sector. On the other hand, the aggressive high-return, high-risk sectors like CD, Bank and Power sectors have turned into rather unattractive low (even negative)-return, high-risk sectors. Thus, crisis has adversely affected the sectors like FMCG, PSU, CD, Bank, Power, and ONG sectors. Of these, perhaps ONG has been the most affected. From an Investor's delight in the pre-crisis period (being the most attractive high-return, low risk sector) it became a high risk sector after the crisis earning negative returns. Metal and CG have been able to avoid the impacts of crisis, while healthcare and automobile emerged as profitable places of investment after the crisis. The crisis has made the IT sector more aggressive in the stock market.

The study thus completes the discussion on designing of profitable investment strategies in BSE. It now proceeds to explore the presence or otherwise of the same for the NSE, the other stock market exchange chosen as the representative of the Indian stock market. The methodologies will remain the same as those used in the previous section.

3.3 Investment Strategies in NSE

As revealed by the exploratory factor analysis, the NSE is characterized by the presence of two uncorrelated, latent structures. The sectors constitute the first and the dominant trend where as the market comes under the second and less dominant structure. Hence, an investor while designing the investment strategy will have to select and combine sectoral and market indexes judiciously. Let us now consider the possible investment strategies under NSE and the impact of crisis on them. The methodologies followed will be the same as those used for the BSE. The sectors, along with the unique risk, will have only one component of systematic risk namely the correlation among the sectoral returns. The market is completely decoupled from the sectors.

3.3.1 Portfolio Construction in NSE: 2005–2012

The sectors are classified in terms of the risk-return relationship. The rankings, Sharpe ratios, extent of systematic risks are shown in Table 3.4.

The sectors are grouped into four in terms of the risk-return relationship. The market is singled out as a high-return, low-risk sector with a positive Sharpe Ratio (rank 5). Risk-averse investors might find the market index as a suitable place for investment.

Table 3.4 Portfolio construction in NSE (2005–2012)

	Sectors	Risk-return relationship	Sharpe ratio ranking	Cross-correlation among sectors
Structure 1	Finance	High return, high risk	4	–
	FMCG	High return low risk	1	Low
	MNC		2	
	Pharmaceuticals		3	
	Commodities	Low return high risk	10	High
	Infrastructure		12	
	Metal		9	
	PSU_Bank		11	
	Energy	Low return low risk	7	Moderate
	IT		8	
	PSE		13	
	Service		6	
Structure 2	Market	High return low risk	5	–

At the sectoral level, the low-return, high-risk group with high systematic risk is very difficult to be accepted by any investor. The low-return, low-risk group with moderate systematic risk, on the other hand, might attract some pessimist investors.

Investment in Sectors: Strategy 1 *Investment in the High return, high risk sector*: Risk-averse investors might find the sector attractive due to its high Sharpe ratio. However, this investment will be preferred by the risk-lovers.

Investment in Sectors: Strategy 2 *Investment in the High return, low risk sector*: The group with very low systematic risk will be a must-pick-up for the risk-averse investors. The choice is further justified by the high Sharpe Ratio ranking of the constituent sectors (rank 1, 2, and 3 respectively).

Investment in Sectors: Strategy 3 *Consideration for high risk independent of level of return:* the investors may think of combining the high-return, high-risk sector (Finance) with the low-return, high-risk sector constituted of Commodities, Infrastructure, Metal, and PSUBanks. This combined group, however, will be preferred by the risk-lover investors.

Investment in Sectors: Strategy 4 *Consideration for high return independent of level of risk:* Investors may think of combining the high-return, high-risk sector (Finance) with the high-return, low-risk sector constituted of FMCG, MNC and Pharmaceuticals. This combined group contains the first four sectors in terms of Sharpe ratio. The risk-averse investors are likely to prefer the portfolio because of the high risk-adjusted return offered by it.

3.3 Investment Strategies in NSE 65

Investment in Sectors: Strategy 5 *Consideration for low risk independent of level of return:* Investors may think of combining the high-return, low-risk sector (constituted of FMCG, MNC and Pharmaceutical) with the low-return, low-risk sector constituted of Energy, IT, PSE, and Services. The risk-averse investors are likely to prefer the portfolio because of the low risk offered by it. However, a closer look at the combined group might reveal that the high-return, low-risk group will always dominate the low-return, low-risk group. This is because the first group contains the first four sectors in terms of Sharpe ratio and has a lower level of systematic risk. Hence, strategy 4 will always be dominated by the strategy 3.

Let us now consider the impact of financial crisis on the investment strategies. For the purpose, we need to compare the investment strategies in the pre- and post-crisis period.

3.3.2 Portfolio Construction in NSE: 2005–2008

The NSE in the pre-crisis period is characterized by presence of three groups at the sectoral level. The high-return, high-risk group, which is often preferred by extreme risk lovers, is absent. The market is singled out as a high-return, low-risk sector with a high and positive Sharpe Ratio (rank 4). Risk-averse investors might find the market index as a suitable place for investment (Table 3.5).

At the sectoral level, the low-return, high-risk sector namely PSU Bank is hardly to be accepted by any. The extreme risk lover might go for it, but it seems unusual. The low Sharpe Ratio for the sector might discourage the risk-averse

Table 3.5 Portfolio construction in NSE: 2005–2008

	Sectors	Risk-return relationship	Cross-correlation among sectors	Sharpe Ratio ranking
Structure 1	Commodity	High return low risk	HIGH	6
	Energy			3
	Finance			2
	Service			1
				5
	PSU bank	Low return high risk	–	10
	FMCG	Low return low risk	LOW	9
	IT			
	MNC			
	Pharmaceuticals			13
	PSE			8
				12
				11
Structure 2	Market	High return low risk	–	4

investor from investing in it. The low-return, low-risk group, with low systematic risk might attract some pessimist investors. The low Sharpe ratios for the individual sectors within the group might be a dispiriting factor.

Investment in Sectors: Strategy 1 *Investment in the High return, low risk sector:* Risk-averse investors will always find the sector attractive. The only uncomfortable factor will be the high systematic risk of the group.

Investment in Sectors: Strategy 2 *Consideration for low risk independent of level of return:* Investors may think of combining the high-return, low-risk sector (constituted of Commodity, Energy, Finance, Infrastructure and Services) with the low-return, low-risk sector constituted of FMCG, IT, MNC, Pharmaceuticals and PSE. The risk-averse investors are likely to prefer the portfolio because of the low risk offered by it. However, a closer look at the combined group might reveal that the high-return, low-risk group will always dominate the low-return, low risk group. This is because the first group contains the sectors with higher Sharpe ratios. Hence, strategy 2 will always be dominated by the strategy 1.

The risk-lovers might find it difficult to single out suitable place for investment.

3.3.3 Portfolio Construction in NSE: 2008–2012

The NSE in the post-crisis period is characterized by presence of four groups at the sectoral level in terms of the risk-return relationship. The market is singled out as a low-return, low-risk sector with a negative Sharpe Ratio. Hence, it is unlikely for the investors to choose the market index as a suitable place for investment (Table 3.6).

At the sectoral level, the low-return, high-risk sector with negative return, negative Sharpe ratio and high systematic risk will hardly be accepted by the investors. Even the most optimistic, risk-loving person will be discouraged to construct his/her portfolio with these sectors. The low-return, low-risk group with low systematic risk will also not find acceptability among investors. This is because of their negative returns and negative Sharpe Ratios. Even the most pessimist investor will avoid the group. The other strategies might be as follows:

Investment in Sectors: Strategy 1 *Investment in the High return, high risk sector:* Risk-averse investors might find the sector attractive due to its high Sharpe ratio. However, this investment will be preferred by the risk-lovers.

Investment in Sectors: Strategy 2 *Investment in the High return, low risk sector:* the group with very low systematic risk will be a must-pick-up for the risk-averse investors. The choice is further justified by the high Sharpe Ratio ranking of the constituent sectors (rank 1, 2 and 3 respectively).

Investment in Sectors: Strategy 3 *Consideration for high return independent of level of risk:* Investors may think of combining the high-return, high-risk sector

3.3 Investment Strategies in NSE 67

Table 3.6 Portfolio construction in NSE: 2008–2012

	Sectors	Risk-return relationship	Cross-correlation among sectors	Sharpe ratio ranking
Structure 1	Finance	High return high risk	High	5
	IT			4
	FMCG	High return low risk	Low	1
	MNC			3
	Pharmaceutical			2
	Commodity	Low return (−) high risk	High	11(−)
	Infrastructure			
	Metal			
	PSU bank			13(−)
				12(−)
				8(−)
	Energy	Low return (−) low risk	Low	9(−)
	PSE			
	Service			10(−)
				7(−)
Structure 2	Market	Low return (-) low risk	–	6(−)

(Finance and IT) with the high-return, low-risk sector constituted of FMCG, MNC and Pharmaceuticals. This combined group contains the first five sectors in terms of Sharpe ratio. The risk-averse investors are likely to prefer the portfolio because of the high risk-adjusted return offered by it. However, in terms of the systematic risk and Sharpe ratio, the first group has a slight edge over the second one. Hence, strategy 3 might be dominated by strategy 2, particularly for some extremely risk-averse investors.

Now we may consider the impact of financial crisis on the investment strategies in NSE. The pre-crisis period was characterized by the absence of high-return, high-risk group. The risk-lovers had relatively fewer choices during the period. The post-crisis period, however, is characterized by low, even negative returns of some sectors making the choice much more limited. Just like the BSE market, IT has transformed itself from a defensive one in the pre-crisis period to an aggressive one in the post-crisis period. Financial sector has become riskier. FMCG, MNC, pharmaceutical have emerged as profitable places for investment, as their return increased after the crisis. Sectors like Commodity, Infrastructure, Metal, PSU bank, Energy, PSE, Services and the market index itself have been adversely affected by the crisis. Their returns became negative after the crisis.

The study thus far has considered the possible investment strategies and portfolio construction in the Indian stock market. Apart from the portfolio construction, the investors often struggle to decide on the optimum holding period for the assets they hold. Often diversification is a risk in itself: by diversifying across more stocks one reduces the specific risks of holding individual stocks and become more vulnerable to the market and economic conditions. Warren Buffet considers diversification as a return management platform, rather than a risk management one. A rational investor should judge financial assets on their merits and their price and should change their allocations as circumstances change. They are to follow a flexible, opportunistic approach that would allow them to invest wherever the expected returns are maximum. According to him, diversification is nothing but a protection against ignorance—"it makes very little sense for those who know what they're doing". It is in this context that the importance of having some knowledge of trading rule crops up.

Reference

Markowitz HM (1952) Portfolio selection. J Financ 7(1):77–91

Chapter 4
Investigation into Optimal Trading Rules in Indian Stock Market

Abstract This chapter deals with momentum trading and possibility of a profitable trading strategy in the Indian stock market. It does so by examining the historical moving averages of the indexes. According to the trading rule, an investor should buy when price is above some moving average of historical prices and sell when price falls below some moving average. The study considers several moving averages, short run, medium run, and long run, and explores whether the general buy and sell strategies fare better than the holding strategy based on the moving average. Existence of a momentum strategy would reaffirm the doubt that the Indian stock market is not efficient. It will put a question mark to the invincibility of the market, as suggested by the efficient market hypothesis.

Keywords Momentum trading · Optimal trading rule · Buy and sell strategy · Moving average · Indian stock market · Efficient market hypothesis

> *"Rule No.1: Never lose money. Rule No.2: Never forget rule No.1"*
>
> Warren Buffett

4.1 Introduction

Efficiency of the financial markets has long been a topic of hot discussion. According to Fama's (1970) efficient market hypothesis, the financial market is inherently efficient, that is, it reflects all available information. Therefore, it is impossible to "beat" the market. In other words, it is impossible for an investor to consistently achieve excess returns on a risk-adjusted basis, given the available information. An efficient market necessarily follows a random walk, or a martingale process. A market following random walk is necessarily impossible to predict. Therefore, it goes perfectly hand-in-hand with the idea that an efficient market is unbeatable. The efficient market hypothesis has been hugely popular

G. Chakrabarti and C. Sen, *Momentum Trading on the Indian Stock Market*, SpringerBriefs in Economics, DOI: 10.1007/978-81-322-1127-3_4, © The Author(s) 2013

since its inception and many modern market models are based on this theory. However, there has been a clear disagreement among economists regarding the efficacy of efficient market hypothesis. Especially after the collapse of the financial market in 2007–2008, the validity of efficient market hypothesis is largely at stake. This study tries to examine the efficiency in Indian stock market by taking 13 sectoral stock indexes from Bombay Stock Exchange and 13 sectoral indexes from National Stock Exchange. The objective of this chapter is to analyze the Indian stock market and figure out a discernible trading rule, which is able to consistently generate a positive return over time, thus "beating" the market. It will be done in three stages. In the first stage, we will try find out the underlying trading rule for all tradable indexes in Bombay Stock Exchange (BSE henceforth) and National Stock Exchange (NSE henceforth). Stage 2 will test the efficacy of the trading rule against the economy's performance. The concluding part of the study will test for volatility contagion across the indexes.

4.2 Literature Review

There is a whole body of empirical research looking into the phenomenon of efficient market and its validity. The evidence suggests that a strongly efficient market is rare, however, most stock markets are largely semistrong efficient. Now this provides the investors with a scope to "beat" the market consistently. Basu (1977) took return data for over 1,400 firms over a period 1956–1971 and considered the price earning ratio for all the firms and concluded that the market behavior is not fully captured by the efficient market hypothesis. The portfolios with low price earning ratios consistently earned superior returns on a risk-adjusted basis, thus making the efficient market hypothesis invalid. Bondt and Thaler (1985) discovered weak for market inefficiency in daily CRSP return data, with a clear January effect. This month-of-year effect, 0 calendar effect has been found to exist in stock market in several studies (*Calendar effects*) are cyclical anomalies in returns, based on different times of year, month or week. Many studies have shown that there is a significant January effect present in many markets. Not only month-of-year effect, calendar effect is witnessed as day of week and even holiday effects are witnessed. Relevant papers include Lakonishok and Smidt (1988), Hawawini and Keim (1995), and Mills and Coutts (1995). Lo and Mackinley (1988) took weekly stock returns to test for efficiency. Their result suggested that the stock market is inherently inefficient and does not follow a random walk. Ding et al. (1993) in their seminal study has shown that the stock market (S&P500) is characterized by long-term memory. If a market exhibits long-term memory, it means that when a shock is propagated into the system, it does not get absorbed by the market instantly, as suggested by the efficient market hypothesis. But it persists into the system for a very long time before slowly disappearing. This is directly in contrast to the efficient market hypothesis. If the market is inefficient or even semi-strong efficient, there may be ways to "beat" the market, i.e., make consistent profits from the market with a suitable buy-sell strategy. The suitable strategy is often guided by looking at the moving averages of the underlying stock. This is called momentum trading. The researchers did not find any suitable literature in momentum trading, as it is mostly applied in businesses.

In recent past, there has been a whole body of literature on possible momentum strategies in the market. Jagadeesh (1990), Lo and MacKinlay (1988), and Fama and French (1988) showed that the market is characterized by negative correlation among stock returns in the long run but positive correlation in the short run, which implies that there is indeed a scope of profitable momentum strategies in the short run. Existence of positive autocorrelation among stocks in the short run and hence relevance of momentum strategies is also documented by Jegadeesh and Titman (1993, 1995). Lee and Swaminathan (2000) documented that momentum strategies are successful in the US stock market. Rouwenhourst (1998) considered 20 emerging stock markets and found significantly positive results when momentum strategies are implemented in all countries. Hameed and Yuanto showed existence of profitable momentum strategies in some selected Asian stock markets. Success of momentum strategies are also documented in the studies of Conrad and Kaul (1998), Richards (1997), and Liu et al. (1999).

4.3 Objectives of the Chapter

1. To find out an optimum trading rule for each index in Indian stock market (BSE and NSE). This will give an insight into how the market can be "beaten". On a more academic note, existence of a trading rule proves that the market is not efficient. The ramification is, manifold.
2. Testing the efficacy of the trading rule across regimes. In other words, whether the same trading rule is applicable during a crisis as well. This will give the investor an insight into whether to stick with the same trading rule when the economy is under considerable economic stress.

The analysis will be done in three stages. The details are given below.

4.4 Dataset

This study will consider all 13 sectoral indexes from BSE, namely BSE CD, BSE POWER, BSE CG, BSE FMCG, BSE TECK, BSE HC, BSE IT, BSE PSU, BSE AUTO, BSE REALTY, BSE METAL, BSE BANKEX, and BSE OIL&GAS. Also, this study will consider all 13 sectoral indexes from NSE, namely CNX AUTO, CNX BANK, CNX ENERGY, CNX FINANCE, CNX FMCG, CNX IT, CNX METALS, CNX MNC, CNX PHARMA, CNX PSU BANK, and S&P CNX

INDUSTRY. The period under the study would be from 2000 till 2011, the data will be taken in a daily basis.

4.5 Finding the Optimum Trading Rule

In the next section, we continue with identifying possible moving average trading rules. According to the trading rule, one buys when price is above some moving average of historical prices and sell when price falls below some moving average.

Methodology

STEP 1 The variable underlying would be the daily return series [where return $= \ln(P_t/P_t - 1)$].

STEP 2 Next, short run, medium run, and long run moving averages are to be constructed.

STEP 3 A general regression model will be constructed which will work as a benchmark for a profitability comparison with trading rule.

STEP 4 All possible combinations of short run, medium run, and long run signals are constructed, such as buy37 (short run combinations); buy314, buy714 (short run–medium run combination); buy330, buy360, buy730, and buy760 (short run–long run combination); buy1430, buy1460, (medium run–long run combination); and buy3060 (long run–long run combination). In reality, an infinite number of combinations can be generated but this study considers till 60 days which, in a high frequency market such as stock market, is significantly long run.

All the buying signals are dummy variable taking a value of 1 if the price is above the nth day moving average of historical prices and zero otherwise.

STEP 5 Regress return on a constant and a lagged value of buy signal. The estimated slope coefficient will give the possible profit. A significantly positive slope coefficient, which is higher than the intercept as well as the coefficient of the general buy sell regression hints toward existence of a profitable trading rule,

STEP 6 All possible buying signals (the set under consideration) are taken into account and the signal with highest profitability shows the optimum trading strategy.

4.6 How the Trading Rule Varies Depending on the Performance of the Economy

The study delves deeper and investigate whether and how the trading rule differs significantly when the economy is experiencing a crisis vis-à-vis when it is performing well.

STEP 1 We divide the whole time series into two periods for each index, namely pre-crisis, and post-crisis period. For this study, we focus mainly on the recent financial crisis of 2008–2010.

STEP 2 Once we have two distinct periods or regimes, we will test for the underlying trading rule for each regime. The target is to identify whether the trading rule during a crisis vary significantly during a time when the economy is performing well.

There are, however, some limitations of this study. For example, (1) the bid—ask spread is not considered, as the data is not available, (2) intraday or tick-by-tick price, rather than daily price would have given a more accurate result, and (3) possible idiosyncrasies may exist, as India is still an emerging market.

4.7 Finding the Optimum Trading Rule for BSE Indexes

Momentum, or in other words, positive serial correlation is a common phenomenon in financial asset returns. According to www.Investopedia.com, "in momentum trading, traders focus on stocks that are moving significantly in one direction on high volume. Momentum traders may hold their positions for a few minutes, a couple of hours or even the entire length of the trading day, depending on how quickly the stock moves and when it changes direction".[1] As the main objective of a momentum trader is to make profit, it is very important from a traders perspective to understand when to ride the momentum train and when to get off it. The most common tool in finding this underlying trading rule is by using the moving average (MA) method.

4.7.1 Visual Analysis of Autocorrelation

An inefficient market is often characterized by long-term memory and traders usually exploit this characteristic to their benefit. Before we move into analyzing the market trend and trading rules, it is beneficial to examine if the underlying series is characterized by long-term memory, or, in other words, whether a shock propagated into the system remains within it for a long time or dies down very quickly. One simple way to test it is checking for autocorrelations. Using the correlogram function, the autocorrelations for each of the 12 return series are generated for 36 lags. Return, is defined at $R_t = \ln(P_t/P_{t-1})$ where P_t is the price on t-th day. Interestingly, even after 36 lags, the autocorrelations do not die down. They still remain significantly greater than zero. The autocorrelation functions are plotted below, in Graphs 4.1, 4.2, 4.3, 4.4, 4.5, 4.6, 4.7, 4.8, 4.9, 4.10, 4.11, and 4.12.

---

[1] http://www.investopedia.com/articles/trading/02/090302.asp#axzz22SMbNkfj

74	4 Investigation into Optimal Trading Rules in Indian Stock Market

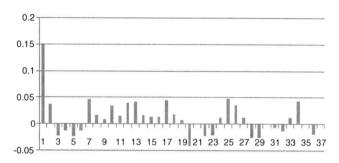

Graph 4.1 ACF for BSE AUTO

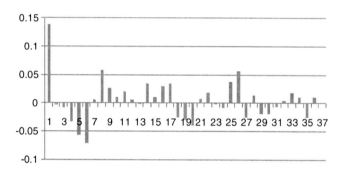

Graph 4.2 ACF for BSE BANK

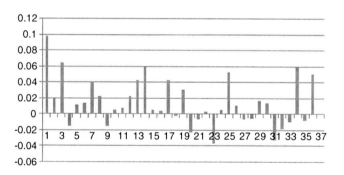

Graph 4.3 ACF for BSE CD

4.7 Finding the Optimum Trading Rule for BSE Indexes

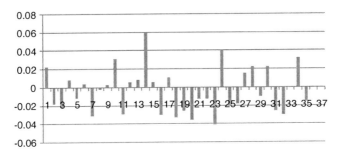

Graph 4.4 ACF for BSE FMCG

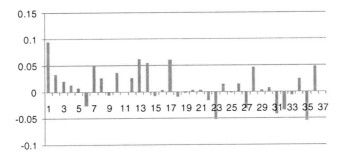

Graph 4.5 ACF for BSE HC

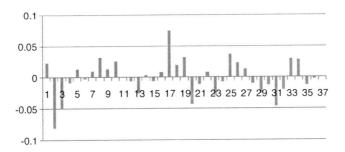

Graph 4.6 ACF for BSE IT

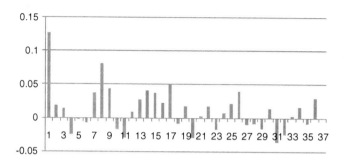

Graph 4.7 ACF for BSE METAL

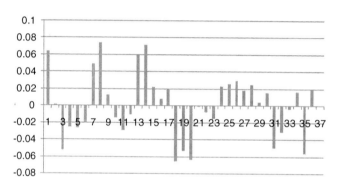

Graph 4.8 ACF for BSE ONG

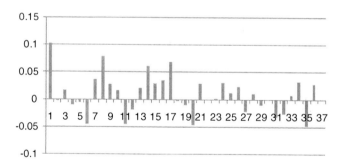

Graph 4.9 ACF for BSE POWER

4.7 Finding the Optimum Trading Rule for BSE Indexes

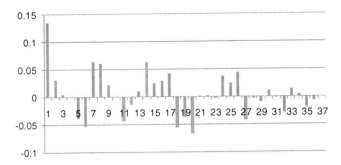

Graph 4.10 ACF for BSE PSU

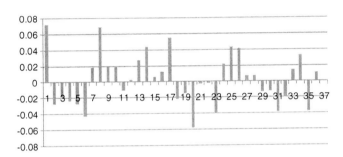

Graph 4.11 ACF for BSE SENSEX

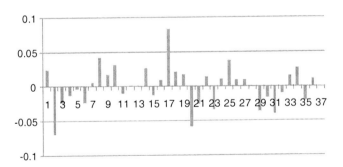

Graph 4.12 ACF for BSE TECK

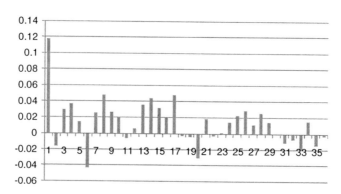

Graph 4.13 ACF for BSE CG

Based on the ACFs above, it can be said that all the return series are characterized by long-term memory, that is, the autocorrelation decays very slowly over a long time. Even after 36 lags, the autocorrelation does not fall to zero. The visual representation above provides some degree of evidence in favor of the market being inefficient (Graph 4.13).

4.7.2 Trading Rule in BSE

The moving averages generated are buy3, buy7, buy14, buy21, buy30, buy60, and all possible combinations of short run, medium run, and long run signals such as buy37 (short run combinations); buy314, buy321, buy714, and buy721 (short run–medium run combination); buy330, buy360, buy730, and buy760 (short run–long run combination); buy1430, buy1460, buy2130, and buy2160 (medium run–medium run combination); and buy3060 (long run–long run combination). Twenty buying signals are also generated. The buying signals are a series of dummy variables which takes a value of 1 when the price is above some specified threshold and zero, when it is below. The buying signals generated are:

1. Buy3 = price > Mov3, i.e., when the return is higher than the 3 days moving average;
2. Buy7 = price > Mov7, i.e., when the return is higher than the 7 days moving average;
3. Buy14 = price > Mov14, i.e., when the return is higher than the 14 days moving average;
4. Buy30 = price > Mov30, i.e., when the return is higher than the 30 days moving average;
5. Buy60 = price > Mov60, i.e., when the return is higher than the 60 days moving average;

4.7 Finding the Optimum Trading Rule for BSE Indexes

6. Buy37 = Mov3 > Mov7, i.e., when the 3 days moving average is higher than the 7 days moving average;
7. Buy314 = Mov3 > Mov14, i.e., when the 3 days moving average is higher than the 14 days moving average;
8. Buy330 = Mov3 > Mov30, i.e., when the 3 days moving average is higher than the 30 days moving average;
9. Buy360 = Mov3 > Mov60, i.e., when the 3 days moving average is higher than the 60 days moving average;
10. Buy714 = Mov7 > Mov14, i.e., when the 7 days moving average is higher than the 14 days moving average;
11. Buy730 = Mov7 > Mov30, i.e., when the 7 days moving average is higher than the 30 days moving average;
12. Buy760 = Mov7 > Mov60, i.e., when the 7 days moving average is higher than the 60 days moving average;
13. Buy1430 = Mov14 > Mov30, i.e., when the 14 days moving average is higher than the 30 days moving average;
14. Buy1460 = Mov14 > Mov60, i.e., when the 14 days moving average is higher than the 60 days moving average; and
15. Buy3060 = Mov30 > Mov60, i.e., when the 30 days moving average is higher than the 60 days moving average

4.7.2.1 Sector 1: BSE AUTO Trading Rule

The daily return of AUTO is regressed upon a constant and the result is summarized in Table 4.1.

In the next step, lagging the buy rule signals by one period, several regression equations are generated. They are

$$AUTO = c + a_1 buy7(-1) \quad AUTO = c + a_2 buy14(-1) \quad AUTO = c + a_3 buy30(-1)$$
$$AUTO = c + a_4 buy60(-1) \quad AUTO = c + a_5 buy714(-1) \quad AUTO = c + a_6 buy730(-1)$$
$$AUTO = c + a_7 buy760(-1) \quad AUTO = c + a_8 buy1430(-1) \quad AUTO = c + a_9 buy1460(-1)$$
$$AUTO = c + a_{10} buy3060(-1)$$

Each regression is estimated and the regression that gives highest daily return, i.e., the coefficient a, is considered. From above regressions, AUTO = $-$ c + $a_3$buy60(-1) gives the highest daily return. The coefficient of BUY60(-1) is 0.0003. This means, when the investor is holding the fund, he is getting a daily return of 0.0003 % and he will be making a loss of 0.0006 % when he is out. The

Table 4.1 Regression result of AUTO on a constant (general buy and sell strategy)

Dependent variable: AUTO				
Variable	Coefficient	Std. error	t-statistic	Prob.
C	0.001	0.000	1.771	0.077

Table 4.2 Regression of AUTO based on the trading rule

Variable	Coefficient	Std. error	t-statistic	Prob.		
C	−0.0006	0.0007	−0.8188	0.4134	R-squared	Adjusted R-squared
BUY60(−1)	0.0003	0.0010	0.2409	0.8097	0.0001	−0.0021

return, however, is small and not so much significant, as seen from the high probability values.

As it can be seen from Table 4.2 above, the profitability of the trading rule is lower than the general daily buy and hold return. This is seen from the fact that the return from the general buy and sell regression is larger and more significant than the return on the best possible trading rule.

4.7.2.2 Sector 2: BSE BANK Trading Rule

The daily return of BANK is regressed upon a constant and the result is summarized below.

The lagged regression equations are

$$BANK = c + a_1 buy7(-1) \quad BANK = c + a_2 buy14(-1) \quad BANK = c + a_3 buy30(-1)$$
$$BANK = c + a_4 buy60(-1) \quad BANK = c + a_5 buy714(-1) \quad BANK = c + a_6 buy730(-1)$$
$$BANK = c + a_7 buy760(-1) \quad BANK = c + a_8 buy1430(-1) \quad BANK = c + a_9 buy1460(-1)$$
$$BANK = c + a_{10} buy3060(-1)$$

From above regressions, $BANK = c + a_3 buy60(-1)$ gives the highest daily return. The result of the regression is summarized in Table 4.4. The coefficient of BUY60(−1) is 0.005 while the intercept coefficient is −0.002. This means, when the investor is holding the fund, he is getting a daily return of 0.0003 % and he will be making a loss of 0.002 % when he is out. The return, is quite significant as well, as seen from the low probability values.

As compared to the general buy and hold pattern in Table 4.3, the trading rule gives a larger return and this return is more statistically significant as well.

Table 4.3 Regression result of BANK on a constant (general buy and sell strategy)

Dependent variable: BANK

Variable	Coefficient	Std. error	t-statistic	Prob.	R-squared	Adjusted R^2
C	0.001	0.000	1.311	0.190	0.000	0.000

Table 4.4 Regression of BANK based on the trading rule

Dependent variable: BANK

Variable	Coefficient	Std. error	t-statistic	Prob.	R^2	Adjusted R^2
C	−0.002	0.001	−2.584	0.010	0.013	0.012
BUY60(−1)	0.005	0.001	4.899	0.000		

4.7 Finding the Optimum Trading Rule for BSE Indexes

Therefore, the optimal trading rule is that the investor must buy whenever the price is higher than the 60 days moving average and do not hold whenever it is below the 60 days moving average (Table 4.4).

4.7.2.3 Sector 3: BSE CD Trading Rule

The daily return of CD is regressed upon a constant and the result is summarized in Table 4.5.

The lagged regression equations are

$$CD = c + a_1 buy7(-1) \qquad CD = c + a_2 buy14(-1) \qquad CD = c + a_3 buy30(-1)$$
$$CD = c + a_4 buy60(-1) \qquad CD = c + a_5 buy714(-1) \qquad CD = c + a_6 buy730(-1)$$
$$CD = c + a_7 buy760(-1) \qquad CD = c + a_8 buy1430(-1) \qquad CD = c + a_9 buy1460(-1)$$
$$CD = c + a_{10} buy3060(-1)$$

From above regressions, $CD = c + a_3 buy60(-1)$ gives the highest daily return. The coefficient of BUY60(−1) is 0.004 and the intercept is −0.001. This means, when the investor is holding the fund, he is getting a daily return of 0.004 % and he will be making a loss of 0.001 % when he is out. The return from the trading rule is statistically significant as well (Table 4.6).

Table 4.5 Regression result of CD on a constant (general buy and sell strategy)

Dependent Variable: CD						
Variable	Coefficient	Std. error	t-statistic	Prob.	R^2	Adjusted R^2
C	0.001	0.000	1.673	0.095	0.000	0.000

Table 4.6 Regression of CD based on the trading rule

Dependent variable: CD						
Variable	Coefficient	Std. error	t-statistic	Prob.	R^2	Adjusted R^2
C	−0.001	0.001	−1.458	0.145	0.008	0.007
BUY60(−1)	0.004	0.001	3.788	0.000		

Comparing the return from the trading rule with the return from the general buy and hold pattern, it can be said that the optimal trading rule is that the investor must buy whenever the price is higher than the 60 days moving average and do not hold whenever it is below the 60 days moving average.

4.7.2.4 Sector 4: BSE FMCG Trading Rule

The daily return of FMCG is regressed upon a constant and the result is summarized in Table 4.7.

82   4 Investigation into Optimal Trading Rules in Indian Stock Market

Table 4.7 Regression result of FMCG on a constant (general buy and sell strategy)

Dependent variable: FMCG

Variable	Coefficient	Std. error	t-statistic	Prob.	R^2	Adjusted R^2
C	0.000853	0.000329	2.596189	0.0095	0.000	0.000

Table 4.8 Regression of FMCG based on the trading rule

Dependent variable: FMCG

Variable	Coefficient	Std. error	t-statistic	Prob.	R^2	Adjusted R^2
C	0.000518	0.000478	1.084459	0.2783	0.000625	0.000089
BUY60(−1)	0.000723	0.000670	1.080065	0.2803		

The lagged regression equations are

$$FMCG = c + a_1 buy7(-1) \qquad FMCG = c + a_2 buy14(-1) \qquad FMCG = c + a_3 buy30(-1)$$
$$FMCG = c + a_4 buy60(-1) \qquad FMCG = c + a_5 buy714(-1) \qquad FMCG = c + a_6 buy730(-1)$$
$$FMCG = c + a_7 buy760(-1) \qquad FMCG = c + a_8 buy1430(-1) \qquad FMCG = c + a_9 buy1460(-1)$$
$$FMCG = c + a_{10} buy3060(-1)$$

From above regressions, $FMCG = c + a_3 buy60(-1)$ gives the highest daily return. The coefficient of $BUY60(-1)$ is 0.000723. This means, when the investor is holding the fund, he is getting a daily return of 0.000723 % and he will be making a smaller profit of 0.000518 % when he is out. The return, however, is small and not so much significant (Table 4.8).

Therefore, the optimal trading rule is that the investor must buy whenever the price is higher than the 60 days moving average and do not hold whenever it is below the 60 days moving average.

4.7.2.5 Sector 5: BSE HC Trading Rule

The daily return of HC is regressed upon a constant and the result is summarized in Table 4.9.

In the next step, lagging the buy rule signals by one period, several regression equations are generated. They are

$$HC = c + a_1 buy7(-1) \qquad HC = c + a_2 buy14(-1) \qquad HC = c + a_3 buy30(-1)$$
$$HC = c + a_4 buy60(-1) \qquad HC = c + a_5 buy714(-1) \qquad HC = c + a_6 buy730(-1)$$
$$HC = c + a_7 buy760(-1) \qquad HC = c + a_8 buy1430(-1) \qquad HC = c + a_9 buy1460(-1)$$
$$HC = c + a_{10} buy3060(-1)$$

Table 4.9 Regression result of HC on a constant (general buy and sell strategy)

Dependent variable: HC

Variable	Coefficient	Std. error	t-statistic	Prob.	R^2	Adjusted R^2
C	0.000465	0.000285	1.631866	0.1029	0.000	0.000

4.7 Finding the Optimum Trading Rule for BSE Indexes

Table 4.10 Regression of HC based on the trading rule

Dependent variable: HC

Variable	Coefficient	Std. error	t-statistic	Prob.	R^2	Adjusted R^2
C	−0.0006	0.0004	−1.4598	0.1445	0.0085	0.0080
BUY60(−1)	0.0023	0.0006	4.0004	0.0001		

From above regressions, $HC = c + a_3 buy60(-1)$ gives the highest daily return. The coefficient of $BUY60(-1)$ is 0.0023 and the intercept is −0.0006. This means, when the investor is holding the fund, he is getting a daily return of 0.0023 % and he will be making a loss of 0.0006 % when he is out. The return is statistically significant as well (Table 4.10).

By comparing the result from the trading rule with the result from the general buy and hold pattern, it can be seen that the return from the trading rule is significantly higher than the return from the general buy and hold strategy. It can be said that the optimal trading rule is that the investor must buy whenever the price is higher than the 60 days moving average and do not hold whenever it is below the 60 days moving average.

4.7.2.6 Sector 6: BSE IT Trading Rule

The daily return of IT is regressed upon a constant and the result is summarized in Table 4.11.

In the next step, lagging the buy rule signals by one period, several regression equations are generated. They are

$IT = c + a_1 buy7(-1)$ $IT = c + a_2 buy14(-1)$ $IT = c + a_3 buy30(-1)$
$IT = c + a_4 buy60(-1)$ $IT = c + a_5 buy714(-1)$ $IT = c + a_6 buy730(-1)$
$IT = c + a_7 buy760(-1)$ $IT = c + a_8 buy1430(-1)$ $IT = c + a_9 buy1460(-1)$
$IT = c + a_{10} buy3060(-1)$

From above regressions, $IT = c + a_3 buy60(-1)$ gives the highest daily return. The coefficient of $BUY60(-1)$ is 0.18 and statistically significant. This means, when the investor is holding the fund, he is getting a daily return of 0.0018 % and he will be making neither a profit nor a loss (or a minutely small and insignificant profit) when he is out (Table 4.12).

Table 4.11 Regression result of IT on a constant (general buy and sell strategy)

Dependent variable: IT

Variable	Coefficient	Std. error	t-statistic	Prob.	R^2	Adjusted R^2
C	0.00045	0.000	0.968	0.333	0.000	0.000

84   4 Investigation into Optimal Trading Rules in Indian Stock Market

Table 4.12 Regression of IT based on the trading rule

Dependent variable: IT

Variable	Coefficient	Std. error	t-statistic	Prob.	R^2	Adjusted R^2
C	0.00	0.00	0.77	0.44	0.000	0.000
Buy60(-1)	0.18	0.18	1.05	0.29		

Therefore, the optimal trading rule is that the investor must buy whenever the price is higher than the 60 days moving average and do not hold whenever it is below the 60 days moving average.

4.7.2.7 Sector 7: BSE Metal Trading Rule

The daily return of METAL is regressed upon a constant and the result is summarized in Table 4.13.

The lagged regression equations are

$$METAL = c + a_1buy7(-1) \qquad METAL = c + a_2buy14(-1) \qquad METAL = c + a_3buy30(-1)$$
$$METAL = c + a_4buy60(-1) \qquad METAL = c + a_5buy714(-1) \qquad METAL = c + a_6buy730(-1)$$
$$METAL = c + a_7buy760(-1) \qquad METAL = c + a_8buy1430(-1) \qquad METAL = c + a_9buy1460(-1)$$
$$METAL = c + a_{10}buy3060(-1)$$

From above regressions, $METAL = c + a_3buy60(-1)$ gives the highest daily return. The coefficient of $BUY60(-1)$ is 0.001 and it is statistically significant as well. This means, when the investor is holding the fund, he is getting a daily return of 0.01 % and he will be making neither a profit nor a loss (or a very small amount of profit) when he is out (Table 4.14).

Therefore, the optimal trading rule is that the investor must buy whenever the price is higher than the 60 days moving average and do not hold whenever it is below the 60 days moving average.

Table 4.13 Regression result of METAL on a constant (general buy and sell strategy)

Dependent variable: METAL

Variable	Coefficient	Std. error	t-statistic	Prob.	R^2	Adjusted R^2
C	0.0003	0.0006	0.4799	0.6314	0.000	0.000

Table 4.14 Regression of METAL based on the trading rule

Dependent variable: METAL

Variable	Coefficient	Std. error	t-statistic	Prob.	R^2	Adjusted R^2
C	0.00	0.00	-2.81	0.00	0.01	0.01
BUY60(-1)	0.01	0.00	4.39	0.00		

4.7 Finding the Optimum Trading Rule for BSE Indexes

4.7.2.8 Sector 8: BSE ONG Trading Rule

The daily return of ONG is regressed upon a constant and the result is summarized in Table 4.15.

In the next step, lagging the buy rule signals by one period, several regression equations are generated. They are

$$ONG = c + a_1 buy7(-1) \qquad ONG = c + a_2 buy14(-1) \qquad ONG = c + a_3 buy30(-1)$$
$$ONG = c + a_4 buy60(-1) \qquad ONG = c + a_5 buy714(-1) \qquad ONG = c + a_6 buy730(-1)$$
$$ONG = c + a_7 buy760(-1) \qquad ONG = c + a_8 buy1430(-1) \qquad ONG = c + a_9 buy1460(-1)$$
$$ONG = c + a_{10} buy3060(-1)$$

Table 4.15 Regression result of ONG on a constant (general buy and sell strategy)

Dependent variable: ONG

Variable	Coefficient	Std. error	t-statistic	Prob.	R^2	Adjusted R^2
C	0.001	0.000	1.158	0.247	0.00	0.00

Table 4.16 Regression of ONG based on the trading rule

Dependent variable: ONG

Variable	Coefficient	Std. error	t-statistic	Prob.	R^2	Adjusted R^2
C	0.000	0.001	−0.639	0.523	0.002	0.002
BUY60(−1)	0.002	0.001	2.133	0.033		

From above regressions, $ONG = c + a_3 buy60(-1)$ gives the highest daily return. The coefficient of BUY60(−1) is 0.002. This means, when the investor is holding the fund, he is getting a daily return of 0.002 % and he will be making a loss of 0.0006 % when he is out. The return, however, is small and not so much significant, as seen from the high probability values (Table 4.16).

The return from the trading rule is significantly higher than the return from the general buy and sell strategy. Therefore, the optimal trading rule is that the investor must buy whenever the price is higher than the 60 days moving average and do not hold whenever it is below the 60 days moving average.

4.7.2.9 Sector 9: BSE Power Trading Rule

The daily return of POWER is regressed upon a constant and the result is summarized in Table 4.17.

Table 4.17 Regression result of POWER on a constant (general buy and sell strategy)

Dependent variable: POWER

Variable	Coefficient	Std. error	t-statistic	Prob.	R^2	Adjusted R^2
C	0.000372	0.000437	0.851265	0.3947	0.0	0.00

86 4 Investigation into Optimal Trading Rules in Indian Stock Market

Table 4.18 Regression of POWER based on the trading rule

Dependent variable: POWER

Variable	Coefficient	Std. error	t-statistic	Prob.	R^2	Adjusted R^2
C	−0.001	0.001	−2.278	0.023	0.008	0.008
BUY60(−1)	0.004	0.001	3.982	0.000		

In the next step, lagging the buy rule signals by one period, several regression equations are generated. They are

$$POWER = c + a_1 buy7(-1) \quad POWER = c + a_2 buy14(-1) \quad POWER = c + a_3 buy30(-1)$$
$$POWER = c + a_4 buy60(-1) \quad POWER = c + a_5 buy714(-1) \quad POWER = c + a_6 buy730(-1)$$
$$POWER = c + a_7 buy760(-1) \quad POWER = c + a_8 buy1430(-1) \quad POWER = c + a_9 buy1460(-1)$$
$$POWER = c + a_{10} buy3060(-1)$$

From above regressions, $POWER = c + a_3 buy60(-1)$ gives the highest daily return. The coefficient of BUY60(−1) is 0.004. This means, when the investor is holding the fund, he is getting a daily return of 0.004 % and he will be making a loss of 0.001 % when he is out (Table 4.18).

The return from the trading rule is significantly higher than the return from the general buy and sell strategy. Therefore, the optimal trading rule is that the investor must buy whenever the price is higher than the 60 days moving average and do not hold whenever it is below the 60 days moving average.

4.7.2.10 Sector 10: BSE PSU Trading Rule

The daily return of PSU is regressed upon a constant and the result is summarized in Table 4.19.

Lagged regression equations are

$$PSU = c + a_1 buy7(-1) \quad PSU = c + a_2 buy14(-1) \quad PSU = c + a_3 buy30(-1)$$
$$PSU = c + a_4 buy60(-1) \quad PSU = c + a_5 buy714(-1) \quad PSU = c + a_6 buy730(-1)$$
$$PSU = c + a_7 buy760(-1) \quad PSU = c + a_8 buy1430(-1) \quad PSU = c + a_9 buy1460(-1)$$
$$PSU = c + a_{10} buy3060(-1)$$

From above regressions, $AUTO = c + a_3 buy60(-1)$ gives the highest daily return. The coefficient of BUY60(−1) is 0.003 and it is statistically significant. This means, when the investor is holding the fund, he is getting a daily return of 0.003 % and he will be making a loss of 0.002 % when he is out (Table 4.20).

Table 4.19 Regression result of PSU on a constant (general buy and sell strategy)

Dependent variable: PSU

Variable	Coefficient	Std. error	t-statistic	Prob.	R^2	Adjusted R^2
C	0.000259	0.00038	0.679893	0.4967	0	0

4.7 Finding the Optimum Trading Rule for BSE Indexes

Table 4.20 Regression of PSU based on the trading rule

Dependent variable: PSU

Variable	Coefficient	Std. error	t-statistic	Prob.	R^2	Adjusted R^2
C	−0.002	0.001	−2.729	0.006	0.011	0.011
BUY60(−1)	0.003	0.001	4.505	0.000		

The optimal trading rule is clearly better in terms of return than the general strategy. Therefore, the optimal trading rule is that the investor must buy whenever the price is higher than the 60 days moving average and do not hold whenever it is below the 60 days moving average.

4.7.2.11 Sector 11: BSE SENSEX Trading Rule

The daily return of SENSEX is regressed upon a constant and the result is summarized in Table 4.21.

In the next step, lagging the buy rule signals by one period, several regression equations are generated. They are

$$SENSEX = c + a_1 buy7(−1) \quad SENSEX = c + a_2 buy14(−1) \quad SENSEX = c + a_3 buy30(−1)$$
$$SENSEX = c + a_4 buy60(−1) \quad SENSEX = c + a_5 buy714(−1) \quad SENSEX = c + a_6 buy730(−1)$$
$$SENSEX = c + a_7 buy760(−1) \quad SENSEX = c + a_8 buy1430(−1) \quad SENSEX = c + a_9 buy1460(−1)$$
$$SENSEX = c + a_{10} buy3060(−1)$$

From above regressions, $SENSEX = c + a_3 buy60(−1)$ gives the highest daily return. The coefficient of BUY60(−1) is 0.002. This means, when the investor is holding the fund, he is getting a daily return of 0.002 % and he will be making a loss of 0.0005 % when he is out (Table 4.22).

Therefore, the optimal trading rule is that the investor must buy whenever the price is higher than the 60 days moving average and do not hold whenever it is below the 60 days moving average.

Table 4.21 Regression result of SENSEX on a constant (general buy and sell strategy)

Dependent variable: SENSEX

Variable	Coefficient	Std. error	t-statistic	Prob.	R^2	Adjusted R^2
C	0.001	0.000	1.378	0.168	0	0

Table 4.22 Regression of SENSEX based on the trading rule

Dependent variable: SENSEX

Variable	Coefficient	Std. error	t-statistic	Prob.	R^2	Adjusted R^2
C	−0.0005	0.001	−0.880	0.379	0.004	0.003
BUY60(−1)	0.002	0.001	2.665	0.008		

4.7.2.12 Sector 12: BSE TECK Trading Rule

The daily return of TECK is regressed upon a constant and the result is summarized in Table 4.23.

The lagged regression equations are

$$TECK = c + a_1 buy7(-1) \qquad TECK = c + a_2 buy14(-1) \qquad TECK = c + a_3 buy30(-1)$$
$$TECK = c + a_4 buy60(-1) \qquad TECK = c + a_5 buy714(-1) \qquad TECK = c + a_6 buy730(-1)$$
$$TECK = c + a_7 buy760(-1) \qquad TECK = c + a_8 buy1430(-1) \qquad TECK = c + a_9 buy1460(-1)$$
$$TECK = c + a_{10} buy3060(-1)$$

Table 4.23 Regression result of TECK on a constant (general buy and sell strategy)

Dependent variable: TECK

Variable	Coefficient	Std. error	t-statistic	Prob.	R^2	Adjusted R^2
C	0.000341	0.000393	0.868616	0.3852	0	0

Table 4.24 Regression of TECK based on the trading rule

Dependent variable: TECK

Variable	Coefficient	Std. error	t-statistic	Prob.	R^2	Adjusted R^2
C	−0.00021	0.001	−0.370	0.712	0.001	0.001
BUY60(−1)	0.001	0.001	1.421	0.155		

From above regressions, $TECK = c + a_3 buy60(-1)$ gives the highest daily return. The coefficient of BUY60(−1) is 0.001. This means, when the investor is holding the fund, he is getting a daily return of 0.001 % and he will be making a loss of 0.00021 % when he is out. The return, however, is small and not so much significant, as seen from the probability values (Table 4.24).

Therefore, the optimal trading rule is that the investor must buy whenever the price is higher than the 60 days moving average and do not hold whenever it is below the 60 days moving average; however, the profitability of the trading rule from is not statistically significant.

Looking at the results above from the study in context of the BSE stocks, one clear pattern emerges. There is a significant amount of inefficiency in the market and there does exist a clear trading rule. For all 13 indexes, the most profitable trading rule emerges in the long run, to be more precise, a buy and sell strategy based on a 60 day moving average is more profitable than a general buy and sell strategy for all indexes.

4.7.2.13 Sector 13: BSE CG Trading Rule

The daily return of BSE CG is regressed upon a constant and the result is summarized in Table 4.25.

4.7 Finding the Optimum Trading Rule for BSE Indexes

Table 4.25 Regression result of CG on a constant (general buy and sell strategy)

Dependent variable: CG

Variable	Coefficient	Std. error	t-statistic	Prob.	R^2	Adjusted R^2
C	0.000341	0.000393	0.868616	0.3852	0	0

Table 4.26 Regression of CG based on the trading rule

Dependent variable: CG

Variable	Coefficient	Std. error	t-statistic	Prob.	R^2	Adjusted R^2
C	−0.001309	0.000493	−2.65334	0.0080	0.012124	0.011808
BUY60(−1)	0.004272	0.000690	6.189957	0.0000		

The lagged regression equations are

$$CG = c + a_1 buy7(-1) \qquad CG = c + a_2 buy14(-1) \qquad CG = c + a_3 buy30(-1)$$
$$CG = c + a_4 buy60(-1) \qquad CG = c + a_5 buy714(-1) \qquad CG = c + a_6 buy730(-1)$$
$$CG = c + a_7 buy760(-1) \qquad CG = c + a_8 buy1430(-1) \qquad CG = c + a_9 buy1460(-1)$$
$$CG = c + a_{10} buy3060(-1)$$

From above regressions, $CG = c + a_3 buy60(-1)$ gives the highest daily return. The coefficient of BUY60(−1) is 0.004272. This means, when the investor is holding the fund, he is getting a statistically significant daily return of 0.004272 % and he will be making a loss of 0.001309 % when he is out (Table 4.26).

Therefore, the optimal trading rule is that the investor must buy whenever the price is higher than the 60 days moving average and do not hold whenever it is below the 60 days moving average, however, the profitability of the trading rule from is not statistically significant.

Looking at the results above from the study in context of the BSE stocks, one clear pattern emerges. There is a significant amount of inefficiency in the market and there does exist a clear trading rule. For all 13 indexes, the most profitable trading rule emerges in the long run, to be more precise, a buy and sell strategy based on a 60 day moving average is more profitable than a general buy and sell strategy for all indexes.

4.8 Finding the Optimum Trading Rule For the NSE Indexes

The study next considers the National Stock exchange and conducts an analysis in the exact similar manner. To save space and avoid repetition, only the regression results are discussed below.

4.8.1 Visual Analysis of Autocorrelation

The analysis starts with the graphical representation of the autocorrelation pattern embedded in each indexes. In the following diagrams, each ACF function is plotted. A close look at the graphs reveal that, like BSE indexes, for NSE indexes as well, the autocorrelation decays slowly and stays significantly different from zero even at long lags (Graphs 4.14, 4.15, 4.16 4.17, 4.18, 4.19, 4.20, 4.21, 4.22, 4.23, 4.24, and 4.25.

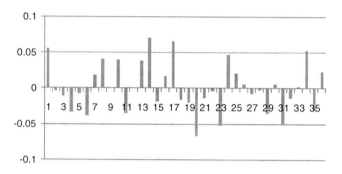

Graph 4.14 ACF for CONSUMPTION

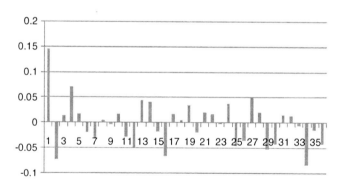

Graph 4.15 ACF for ENERGY

4.8 Finding the Optimum Trading Rule For the NSEIndexes

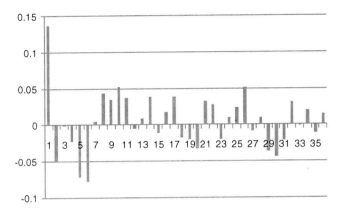

Graph 4.16 ACF for FINANCE

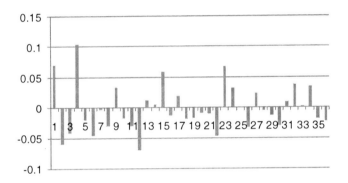

Graph 4.17 ACF for FMCG

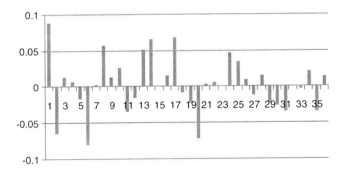

Graph 4.18 ACF for INFRA

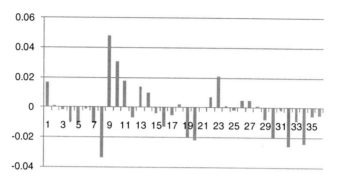

Graph 4.19 ACF for IT

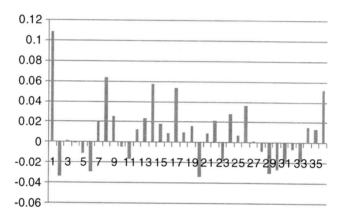

Graph 4.20 ACF for METAL

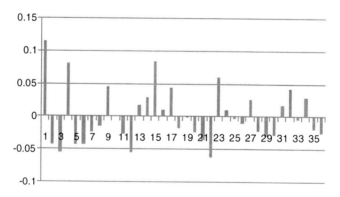

Graph 4.21 ACF for MNC

4.8 Finding the Optimum Trading Rule For the NSEIndexes

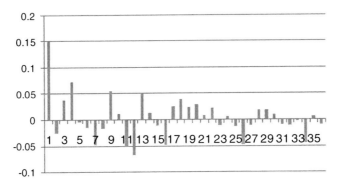

Graph 4.22 ACF for PHARMA

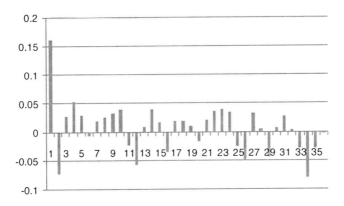

Graph 4.23 ACF for PSE

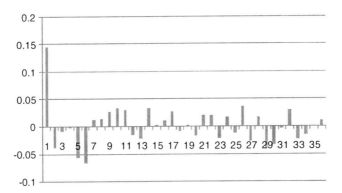

Graph 4.24 ACF for PSU

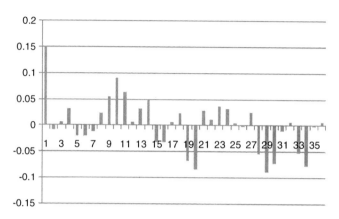

Graph 4.25 ACF for SERVICE

4.8.2 Trading Rule in NSE

4.8.2.1 Sector 1: NSE Consumption Trading Rule

The regression result for general buy and sell strategy is summarized in Table 4.27.

The trading rule that returns the highest profit is based on 60 days moving average. The regression result for a 60 day trading rule is given in Table 4.28.

The coefficient of BUY60(−1) is 0.0015. This implies, when the investor is holding the fund, he is getting a daily return of 0.0015 % and he will be making a loss of 0.00055 % when he is out. The return from the general buy and sell strategy is 0.000361. The return from the trading rule is clearly better than the general strategy. Therefore, the optimal trading rule is that the investor must buy whenever the price is higher than the 60 days moving average and do not hold whenever it is below the 60 days moving average.

Table 4.27 Regression result of NSE Consumption on a constant (general buy and sell strategy)

Dependent variable: Consumption

Variable	Coefficient	Std. error	t-statistic	Prob.	R^2	Adjusted R^2
C	0.000361	0.000417	0.865903	0.3867	0	0

Table 4.28 Regression of NSE Consumption based on the trading rule

Dependent variable: Consumption

Variable	Coefficient	Std. error	t-statistic	Prob.	R^2	Adjusted R^2
C	−0.00055	0.000609	−0.91092	0.3625	0.002248	0.001548
BUY60(−1)	0.001544	0.000862	1.79127	0.0735		

4.8.2.2 Sector 2: NSE Energy Trading Rule

The daily return of ENERGY is regressed upon a constant and the result is summarized in Table 4.29.

The best trading rule for NSE ENERGY is based on 60 day moving average. The regression output is provided in Table 4.30.

Table 4.29 Regression result of NSE Energy on a constant (general buy and sell strategy)

Dependent variable: ENERGY

Variable	Coefficient	Std. error	t-statistic	Prob.	R^2	Adjusted R^2
C	−0.00119	0.000448	−2.64791	0.0082	0	0

Table 4.30 Regression of NSE Energy based on the trading rule

Dependent variable: ENERGY

Variable	Coefficient	Std. error	t-statistic	Prob.	R^2	Adjusted R^2
C	−0.00296	0.000632	−4.68134	0	0.011826	0.011132
BUY60(−1)	0.003732	0.000904	4.128144	0		

The coefficient of BUY60(−1) is 0.0037. This implies, when the investor is holding the fund, he is earning a daily return of 0.0015 % and he will be making a loss of 0.00296 % when he is out. The return from the general buy and sell strategy is a 0.00119 loss. The return from the trading rule is clearly better than the general strategy. Therefore, the optimal trading rule is that the investor must buy whenever the price is higher than the 60 days moving average and do not hold whenever it is below the 60 days moving average.

4.8.2.3 Sector 3: NSE Finance Trading Rule

The daily return of NSE FINANCE is regressed upon a constant and the result is summarized in Table 4.31.

The best trading rule for NSE FINANCE is based on 60 day moving average as well. The regression output is provided in Table 4.32.

The coefficient of BUY60(−1) is 0.00446. This means, when the investor is holding the fund, he is getting a daily return of 0.00446 % and he will be making a loss of 0.00143 % when he is out. The return from the general buy and sell strategy is 0.000836. The return from the trading rule is clearly better than the general

Table 4.31 Regression result of NSE Finance on a constant (general buy and sell strategy)

Dependent variable: FINANCE

Variable	Coefficient	Std. error	t-statistic	Prob.	R^2	Adjusted R^2
C	0.000836	0.000618	1.352785	0.1763	0	0

4 Investigation into Optimal Trading Rules in Indian Stock Market

Table 4.32 Regression of NSE Finance based on the trading rule

Dependent variable: FINANCE

Variable	Coefficient	Std. error	t-statistic	Prob.	R^2	Adjusted R^2
C	−0.00143	0.000903	−1.58079	0.1141	0.008683	0.007987
BUY60(−1)	0.004459	0.001263	3.531701	0.0004		

strategy. Therefore, the optimal trading rule is that the investor must buy whenever the price is higher than the 60 days moving average and do not hold whenever it is below the 60 days moving average.

4.8.2.4 Sector 4: NSE FMCG Trading Rule

The daily return of FMCG is regressed upon a constant and the result is summarized in Table 4.33.

Table 4.33 Regression result of NSE FMCG on a constant (general buy and sell strategy)

Dependent variable: FMCG

Variable	Coefficient	Std. error	t-statistic	Prob.	R^2	Adjusted R^2
C	0.00021	0.0004	0.53488	0.5928	0	0

Table 4.34 Regression of NSE FMCG based on the trading rule

Dependent variable: FMCG

Variable	Coefficient	Std. error	t-statistic	Prob.	R^2	Adjusted R^2
C	−0.0011	0.00054	−1.9995	0.0457	0.008069	0.007372
BUY60(−1)	0.00259	0.00076	3.40344	0.0007		

The best trading rule for NSE FMCG is based on 60 day moving average. The regression output is provided in Table 4.34.

The coefficient of BUY60(−1) is 0.00259. This implies, when the investor is holding the fund, he is getting a daily return of 0.00259 % and he will be making a loss of 0.00109 % when he is out. The return from the general buy and sell strategy is 0.000212. The return from the trading rule is clearly better than the general strategy. Therefore, the optimal trading rule is that the investor must buy whenever the price is higher than the 60 days moving average and do not hold whenever it is below the 60 days moving average.

4.8.2.5 Sector 5: NSE INFRA Trading Rule

The daily return of INFRA is regressed upon a constant and the result is summarized in Table 4.35.

4.8 Finding the Optimum Trading Rule For the NSEIndexes 97

Table 4.35 Regression result of NSE INFRA on a constant (general buy and sell strategy)

Dependent variable: INFRA

Variable	Coefficient	Std. error	t-statistic	Prob.	R^2	Adjusted R^2
C	0.00082	0.00057	1.4347	0.1516	0	0

Table 4.36 Regression of NSE INFRA based on the trading rule

Dependent variable: INFRA

Variable	Coefficient	Std. error	R^2	Adjusted R^2
C	−0.0008	0.00084	0.00453	0.00384
BUY60(−1)	0.00296	0.00116		

The best trading rule for NSE INFRA is based on 60 day moving average. The regression output is provided in Table 4.36.

The coefficient of BUY60(−1) is 0.00296. This means, when the investor is holding the fund, he is getting a daily return of 0.00296 % and he will be making a loss of 0.00077 % when he is out. The return from the general buy and sell strategy is 0.00082. The return from the trading rule is clearly better than the general strategy. Therefore, the optimal trading rule is that the investor must buy whenever the price is higher than the 60 days moving average and do not hold whenever it is below the 60 days moving average.

4.8.2.6 Sector 6: NSE IT Trading Rule

The daily return of IT is regressed upon a constant and the result is summarized in Table 4.37.

The best trading rule for NSE IT is based on 14 day moving average. The regression output is provided in Table 4.38.

Table 4.37 Regression result of NSE IT on a constant (general buy and sell strategy)

Dependent variable: IT

Variable	Coefficient	Std. error	t-statistic	Prob.	R^2	Adjusted R^2
C	−0.0017	0.00178	−0.9522	0.3412	0	0

Table 4.38 Regression of NSE IT based on the trading rule

Dependent variable: IT

Variable	Coefficient	Std. error	t-statistic	Prob.	R^2	Adjusted R^2
C	0.00052	0.00267	0.19443	0.8459	0.001265	0.000564
BUY60(−1)	−0.005	0.00369	−1.343	0.1795		

The coefficient of BUY60(−1) is 0.00126. This means, when the investor is holding the fund, he is getting a daily return of 0.00126 % and he will be making a loss of 0.00052 % when he is out. The return from the general buy and sell strategy is a loss of 0.0017. The return from the trading rule is clearly better than the general strategy. Therefore, the optimal trading rule is that the investor must buy whenever the price is higher than the 60 days moving average and do not hold whenever it is below the 60 days moving average.

4.8.2.7 Sector 7: NSE METAL Trading Rule

The daily return of METAL is regressed upon a constant and the result is summarized in Table 4.39.

The best trading rule for NSE METAL is based on 60 day moving average. The regression output is provided in Table 4.40.

Table 4.39 Regression result of NSE METAL on a constant (general buy and sell strategy)

Dependent variable: METAL

Variable	Coefficient	Std. error	t-statistic	Prob.	R^2	Adjusted R^2
C	0.00098	0.00075	1.3117	0.1898	0	0

Table 4.40 Regression of NSE METAL based on the trading rule

Dependent variable: METAL

Variable	Coefficient	Std. error	t-statistic	Prob.	R^2	Adjusted R^2
C	−0.0012	0.00109	−1.0849	0.2782	0.006603	0.005906
BUY60(−1)	0.00469	0.00152	3.07661	0.0021		

The coefficient of BUY60(−1) is 0.004687. This implies, when the investor is holding the fund, he is getting a daily return of 0.004687 % and he will be making a loss of 0.00118 % when he is out. The return from the general buy and sell strategy is 0.000983. The return from the trading rule is clearly better than the general strategy. Therefore, the optimal trading rule is that the investor must buy whenever the price is higher than the 60 days moving average and do not hold whenever it is below the 60 days moving average.

4.8.2.8 Sector 8: NSE MNC Trading Rule

The daily return of MNC is regressed upon a constant and the result is summarized in Table 4.41.

4.8 Finding the Optimum Trading Rule For the NSEIndexes

Table 4.41 Regression result of NSE MNC on a constant (general buy and sell strategy)

Dependent variable: MNC

Variable	Coefficient	Std. error	t-statistic	Prob.	R^2	Adjusted R^2
C	0.0002	0.00037	0.55338	0.5801	0	0

Table 4.42 Regression of NSE MNC based on the trading rule

Dependent variable: MNC

Variable	Coefficient	Std. error	t-statistic	Prob.	R^2	Adjusted R^2
C	−0.001	0.00051	−2.0044	0.0452	0.009039	0.008343
BUY60(−1)	0.00257	0.00071	3.60407	0.0003		

The best trading rule for NSE MNC is based on 60 day moving average. The regression output is provided in Table 4.42.

The coefficient of BUY60(−1) is 0.00257. This means, when the investor is holding the fund, he is earning a daily return of 0.00257 % and he will be making a loss of 0.00103 % when he is out. The return from the general buy and sell strategy is 0.000204. The return from the trading rule is clearly better than the general strategy. Therefore, the optimal trading rule is that the investor must buy whenever the price is higher than the 60 days moving average and do not hold whenever it is below the 60 days moving average.

4.8.2.9 Sector 9: NSE PHARMA Trading Rule

The daily return of PHARMA is regressed upon a constant and the result is summarized in Table 4.43.

The best trading rule for NSE PHARMA is based on 60 day moving average. The regression output is provided in Table 4.44.

Table 4.43 Regression result of NSE PHARMA on a constant (general buy and sell strategy)

Dependent variable: PHARMA

Variable	Coefficient	Std. error	t-statistic	Prob.	R^2	Adjusted R^2
C	0.00068	0.00034	1.9884	0.047	0	0

Table 4.44 Regression of NSE PHARMA based on the trading rule

Dependent variable: PHARMA

Variable	Coefficient	Std. error	t-statistic	Prob.	R^2	Adjusted R^2
C	−0.0011	0.00049	−2.2022	0.0278	0.018301	0.017611
BUY60(−1)	0.0035	0.00068	5.15227	0		

The coefficient of BUY60(−1) is 0.00349. This means, when the investor is holding the fund, he is getting a daily return of 0.00349 % and he will be making a loss of 0.00109 % when he is out. The return from the general buy and sell strategy is 0.000675. The return from the trading rule is clearly better than the general strategy. Therefore, the optimal trading rule is that the investor must buy whenever the price is higher than the 60 days moving average and do not hold whenever it is below the 60 days moving average.

4.8.2.10 Sector 10: NSE PSE Trading Rule

The daily return of PSE is regressed upon a constant and the result is summarized in Table 4.45.

The best trading rule for NSE PSE is based on 60 day moving average. The regression output is provided in Table 4.46.

Table 4.45 Regression result of NSE PSE on a constant (general buy and sell strategy)

Dependent variable: PSE

Variable	Coefficient	Std. error	t-statistic	Prob.	R^2	Adjusted R^2
C	0.00077	0.00051	1.51716	0.1294	0	0

Table 4.46 Regression of NSE PSE based on the trading rule

Dependent variable: PSE

Variable	Coefficient	Std. error	t-statistic	Prob.	R^2	Adjusted R^2
C	−0.0012	0.00072	−1.724	0.0849	0.01298	0.01229
BUY60(−1)	0.00437	0.00101	4.32798	0		

The coefficient of BUY60(−1) is 0.0044. This means, when the investor is holding the fund, he is getting a daily return of 0.0044 % and he will be making a loss of 0.00124 % when he is out. The return from the general buy and sell strategy is 0.000765. The return from the trading rule is clearly better than the general strategy. Therefore, the optimal trading rule is that the investor must buy whenever the price is higher than the 60 days moving average and do not hold whenever it is below the 60 days moving average.

4.8.2.11 Sector 11: NSE PSU Trading Rule

The daily return of PSU is regressed upon a constant and the result is summarized in Table 4.47.

The best trading rule for NSE PSU is based on 60 day moving average. The regression output is provided in Table 4.48.

4.8 Finding the Optimum Trading Rule For the NSEIndexes

Table 4.47 Regression result of NSE PSU on a constant (general buy and sell strategy)

Dependent variable: PSU

Variable	Coefficient	Std. error	t-statistic	Prob.	R^2	Adjusted R^2
C	0.00078	0.00066	1.18467	0.2363	0	0

Table 4.48 Regression of NSE PSU based on the trading rule

Dependent variable: PSU

Variable	Coefficient	Std. error	t-statistic	Prob.	R^2	Adjusted R^2
C	−0.0017	0.00095	−1.7586	0.0789	0.0089	0.00821
BUY60(−1)	0.00478	0.00134	3.57663	0.0004		

The coefficient of BUY60(−1) is 0.004775. This means, when the investor is holding the fund, he is earning a daily return of 0.004775 % and he will be making a loss of 0.00167 % when he is out. The return from the general buy and sell strategy is 0.000783. The return from the trading rule is clearly better than the general strategy. Therefore, the optimal trading rule is that the investor must buy whenever the price is higher than the 60 days moving average and do not hold whenever it is below the 60 days moving average.

4.8.2.12 Sector 12: NSE SERVICE Trading Rule

The daily return of SERVICE is regressed upon a constant and the result is summarized in Table 4.49.

The best trading rule for NSE SERVICE is based on 60 day moving average. The regression output is provided in Table 4.50.

The coefficient of BUY60(−1) is 0.003969. This means, when the investor is holding the fund, he is earning a daily return of 0.003969 % and he will be making a loss of 0.0021 % when he is out. The return from the general buy and sell strategy is a loss of 0.0017. The return from the trading rule is clearly better than

Table 4.49 Regression result of NSE SERVICE on a constant (general buy and sell strategy)

Dependent variable: SERVICE

Variable	Coefficient	Std. error	t-statistic	Prob.	R^2	Adjusted R^2
C	0.00021	0.00059	0.35445	0.7231	0	0

Table 4.50 Regression of NSE SERVICE based on the trading rule

Dependent variable: SERVICE

Variable	Coefficient	Std. error	t-statistic	Prob.	R^2	Adjusted R^2
C	−0.0021	0.00085	−2.4692	0.0137	0.00803	0.00733
BUY60(−1)	0.00397	0.00117	3.39481	0.0007		

the general strategy. Therefore, the optimal trading rule is that the investor must buy whenever the price is higher than the 60 days moving average and do not hold whenever it is below the 60 days moving average.

So far, the analysis suggests the Indian stock market is quite risk averse in nature, as the holding pattern of stocks is determined by a 60 day moving average, that is a long run in stock market. The next section is devoted in the investigation of the fact whether the market has become more risk averse after the recent crisis or it was always like this. For this purpose, a similar methodology is applied before and after the crisis in order to understand any discernible change in the trading rule.

4.9 Behavior of Indexes Before and After the Crisis

4.9.1 Behavior of NSE Indexes Before and After the Crisis

This section segments the return of NSE indexes before and after the financial crisis. The pre-crisis period is considered to be January 2005 to January 2008 and the post-crisis period is considered to be February 2008 till September 2012.

4.9.1.1 Behavior of NSE Indexes in the Pre-Crisis Period

The results of the general buy and sell strategy for all the indexes are summarized in Tables 4.51 and 4.52.

As the result above suggests, the 60 day trading rule is almost always more profitable for the investor, except for the case of NSE INFRA, where the general buy and sell strategy is more profitable. But the majority of the indexes show a clear trading pattern, which is based on a 60 day moving average of the stock price.

In the next section, we analyze the pattern for the post-crisis period, starting from February 2008 till September 2012.

Table 4.51 General buy and sell strategy in NSE in pre-crisis period

Sector	Variable	Coefficient	Std. error	t-statistic	Prob.	R^2	Adjusted R^2
Consumption	C	0.000882	0.000731	1.206755	0.2281	0	0
Energy	C	0.001165	0.000602	1.935092	0.0533	0	0
Finance	C	0.001493	0.000654	2.284808	0.0226	0	0
FMCG	C	0.00092	0.000561	1.639455	0.1015	0	0
Infrastructure	C	0.001621	0.000636	2.549451	0.011	0	0
IT	C	0.000346	0.000603	0.574046	0.5661	0	0
Metal	C	0.001666	0.000931	1.790747	0.0737	0	0
MNC	C	0.000914	0.000516	1.773189	0.0766	0	0
Pharmaceutical	C	0.000248	0.000497	0.498762	0.2907	0	0
PSE	C	0.000808	0.000617	1.309682	0.1907	0	0
PSU Bank	C	0.000988	0.000763	1.294345	0.1959	0	0
Service	C	0.001084	0.000575	1.885693	0.0597	0	0

4.9 Behavior of Indexes Before and After the Crisis

Table 4.52 Trading rule in NSE in pre-crisis period

Sector	Variable	Coefficient	Std. error	t-statistic	Prob.	R^2	Adjusted R^2
Consumption	C	−0.0004	0.0012	−0.3039	0.7613	0.0023	0.0001
	BUY60(−1)	0.0017	0.0016	1.0196	0.3085		
Energy	C	0.0004	0.0009	0.4506	0.6524	0.0024	0.001
	BUY60(−1)	0.0017	0.0013	1.3147	0.189		
Finance	C	−0.001	0.001	−1.0048	0.3153	0.0191	0.0177
	BUY60(−1)	0.005	0.0014	3.7187	0.0002		
FMCG	C	0.0005	0.0009	0.5308	0.5957	0.0012	−0.0002
	BUY60(−1)	0.0011	0.0012	0.9285	0.3535		
Infrastructure	C	0.0005	0.001	0.5038	0.6146	0.005	0.0036
	BUY60(−1)	0.0025	0.0013	1.8869	0.0596		
IT	C	0.00000	0.0009	−0.0504	0.9598	0.0009	−0.0005
	BUY60(−1)	0.001	0.0013	0.7966	0.426		
Metal	C	0.0003	0.0014	0.2301	0.8181	0.0032	0.0018
	BUY60(−1)	0.003	0.002	1.5036	0.1331		
MNC	C	−0.0004	0.0008	−0.4884	0.6254	0.0085	0.0071
	BUY60(−1)	0.0027	0.0011	2.4616	0.0141		
Pharmaceutical	C	−0.0007	0.0008	−0.9651	0.3348	0.007	0.0056
	BUY60(−1)	0.0023	0.001	2.2311	0.026		
PSE	C	−0.0008	0.001	−0.8516	0.3947	0.009	0.0076
	BUY60(−1)	0.0033	0.0013	2.539	0.0113		
PSU Bank	C	0.001	0.0008	1.2055	0.2284	0.0002	−0.0012
	BUY60(−1)	0.0705	0.1913	0.3686	0.7126		
Service	C	−0.0001	0.0009	−0.1504	0.8805	0.0072	0.0058
	BUY60(−1)	0.0027	0.0012	2.2711	0.0234		

4.9.1.2 Behavior of NSE Indexes in the Post-Crisis Period

The results of the general buy and sell strategy and trading rules for all the indexes are summarized in Table 4.53 and 4.54.

Table 4.53 General buy and sell strategy in NSE in post-crisis period

Sector	Variable	Coefficient	Std. error	t-statistic	Prob.	R^2	Adjusted R^2
Consumption	C	0.0001	0.0005	0.1568	0.8755	0	0
Energy	C	−0.00027	0.00062	−0.43085	0.6667	0	0
Finance	C	−0.00016	0.000789	−0.20487	0.8377	0	0
FMCG	C	0.00061	0.000452	1.348498	0.1778	0	0
Infrastructure	C	−0.00084	0.000686	−1.22757	0.2199	0	0
IT	C	0.000487	0.00068	0.716013	0.4742	0	0
Metal	C	−0.00054	0.000852	−0.63602	0.5249	0	0
MNC	C	0.00026	0.000477	0.545315	0.5857	0	0
Pharmaceutical	C	0.000562	0.000433	1.296921	0.195	0	0
PSE	C	−0.00025	0.00056	−0.45353	0.6503	0	0
PSU Bank	C	−0.00014	0.000773	−0.1835	0.8544	0	0
Service	C	−0.00011	0.000635	−0.17599	0.8603	0	0

Table 4.54 Trading rule in NSE in post-crisis period

Sector	Variable	Coefficient	Std. error	t-statistic	Prob.	R^2	Adjusted R^2
Consumption	C	−0.0008	0.000713	−1.12621	0.2604	0.003243	0.002139
	BUY60(−1)	0.001768	0.001032	1.714017	0.0869		
Energy	C	−0.00122	0.000863	−1.41596	0.1571	0.002277	0.001172
	BUY60(−1)	0.001788	0.001246	1.435438	0.1515		
Finance	C	−0.00212	0.001124	−1.8816	0.0602	0.007682	0.006583
	BUY60(−1)	0.004202	0.001589	2.643886	0.0083		
FMCG	C	−1.74E − 05	0.000642	−0.02706	0.9784	0.001691	0.000585
	BUY60(−1)	0.001131	0.000914	1.236598	0.2166		
Infrastructure	C	−0.00176	0.00099	−1.77596	0.0761	0.00193	0.000821
	BUY60(−1)	0.001836	0.001391	1.319118	0.1875		
IT	C	0.000259	0.000957	0.270888	0.7865	0.00294	0.00254
	BUY60(−1)	0.000191	0.001365	0.140094	0.8886		
Metal	C	−0.00368	0.001228	−2.99379	0.0028	0.013946	0.012854
	BUY60(−1)	0.006171	0.001727	3.573673	0.0004		
MNC	C	−1.03E − 05	0.000685	−0.01503	0.988	0.000267	−0.00084
	BUY60(−1)	0.000478	0.000974	0.491431	0.6232		
Pharmaceutical	C	−0.00081	0.000617	−1.31921	0.1874	0.00813	0.007031
	BUY60(−1)	0.002401	0.000883	2.72053	0.0066		
PSE	C	−0.00107	0.000774	−1.38725	0.1657	0.002431	0.001326
	BUY60(−1)	0.001655	0.001116	1.483342	0.1383		
PSU Bank	C	−0.00289	0.001115	−2.59218	0.0097	0.014762	0.013658
	BUY60(−1)	0.005727	0.001567	3.655833	0.0003		
Service	C	−0.00079	0.000913	−0.85968	0.3902	0.001247	0.000141
	BUY60(−1)	0.001365	0.001285	1.061977	0.2885		

4.9 Behavior of Indexes Before and After the Crisis

The post-crisis period behavior of the NSE indexes, surprisingly exhibit a similar trading pattern. Except NSE IT, all other indexes have a clear trading rule, that says when price goes above 60 day moving average, the investor should hold to make profit. Only for NSE IT, the general buy and sell strategy is applicable.

Let us now move on to consider the presence or otherwise of the trading rule in Bombay Stock Exchange. A comparison between NSE and BSE would enable us to get a comprehensive picture of the Indian stock market.

4.9.2 Behavior of BSE Indexes Before and After the Crisis

This section segments the return of BSE indexes before and after the financial crisis. The pre-crisis period is considered to be January 2005 to January 2008 and the post-crisis period is considered to be February 2008 till September 2012.

4.9.2.1 Behavior of BSE Indexes in the Pre-Crisis Period

The general buying and selling rule for different sectoral and market indexes in the BSE in the pre-crisis period is described in Table 4.55.

The trading strategies in BSE are shown in Table 4.56.

The result above suggests that except BSE OILGAS, all other indexes show a clear pattern of profitable trading policy. For each one of the indexes, except OILGAS, the 60 day moving average presents a profitable holding pattern than the general buy and sells strategy.

Table 4.55 General buy and sell strategy in BSE in pre-crisis period

Sector	Variable	Coefficient	Std. error	t-statistic	Prob.	R^2	Adjusted R^2
FMCG	C	0.000921	0.000565	1.631074	0.1033	0	0
CD	C	0.001531	0.000717	2.135051	0.0331	0	0
HC	C	0.000207	0.000485	0.427633	0.669	0	0
Auto	C	0.000662	0.000558	1.185604	0.2361	0	0
Power	C	0.001709	0.000652	2.621872	0.0089	0	0
IT	C	0.000434	0.000608	0.71367	0.4756	0	0
Metal	C	0.001154	0.000818	1.410816	0.1587	0	0
ONG	C	0.001559	0.000645	2.415678	0.0159	0	0
TecK	C	0.0008	0.000575	1.390436	0.1648	0	0
PSU	C	0.000774	0.000598	1.294125	0.196	0	0
Bank	C	0.001358	0.000668	2.032077	0.0425	0	0
SENSEX	C	0.001259	0.00054	2.329539	0.0201	0	0
CG	C	0.000732	0.000501	1.461662	0.1441	0	0

Table 4.56 Trading rule in BSE in pre-crisis period

Sector	Variable	Coefficient	Std. error	t-statistic	Prob.	R^2	Adjusted R^2
FMCG	C	0.000445	0.00086	0.517534	0.6049	0.001185	−0.00022
	BUY60(−1)	0.001094	0.001192	0.917608	0.3591		
CD	C	1.16E − 05	0.001045	0.011093	0.9912	0.007561	0.006163
	BUY60(−1)	0.003443	0.00148	2.325753	0.0203		
HC	C	−0.00116	0.000745	−1.56063	0.1191	0.012678	0.011287
	BUY60(−1)	0.00307	0.001017	3.01942	0.0026		
Auto	C	−0.001	0.000852	−1.17318	0.2411	0.0124	0.011009
	BUY60(−1)	0.003505	0.001174	2.985747	0.0029		
Power	C	0.001278	0.000958	1.334157	0.1826	0.001098	−0.00031
	BUY60(−1)	0.001223	0.001384	0.883314	0.3774		
IT	C	−0.00017	0.000888	−0.19562	0.845	0.001428	0.000022
	BUY60(−1)	0.001293	0.001284	1.007625	0.314		
Metal	C	0.000122	0.001205	0.101603	0.9191	0.002534	0.001129
	BUY60(−1)	0.002338	0.001741	1.343092	0.1797		
ONG	C	0.001451	0.000952	1.525096	0.1277	0.000313	−0.0011
	BUY60(−1)	0.000648	0.001375	0.47114	0.6377		
TecK	C	0.000267	0.000838	0.317988	0.7506	0.001663	0.000257
	BUY60(−1)	0.001317	0.001211	1.087552	0.2772		
PSU	C	5.47E − 05	0.000871	0.062779	0.95	0.002905	0.001501
	BUY60(−1)	0.001811	0.001259	1.438353	0.1508		
Bank	C	−0.00112	0.000979	−1.13886	0.2551	0.018847	0.017465
	BUY60(−1)	0.005121	0.001387	3.693057	0.0002		
SENSEX	C	0.000629	0.000793	0.793894	0.4275	0.001563	0.000237
	BUY60(−1)	0.001619	0.001145	1.413165	0.158		
CG	C	−0.000728	0.000728	−1.00023	0.3174	0.011051	0.010222
	BUY60(−1)	0.003662	0.001003	3.652635	0.0003		

4.9.2.2 Behavior of BSE Indexes in the Post-Crisis Period

The general buying and selling rule for different sectoral and market indexes in the BSE in the post-crisis period is described in table 4.57.

The trading strategies in post-crisis BSE are shown in Table 4.58.

A look at the results from the post-crisis SENSEX indexes show that largely the market exhibits a long term holding pattern. Out of the 12 indexes, only one index, FMCG does not show a profitable trading rule. Ten of the remaining eleven indexes exhibit a profitable trading rule based on a 60 day moving average and IT shows a profitable trading rule at 30 day moving average. Therefore, it can be concluded that the Indian stock market is quite pessimistic and risk averse, because even after the crisis, the trading pattern does not change much.

4.9 Behavior of Indexes Before and After the Crisis

Table 4.57 General buy and sell strategy in BSE in post-crisis period

Sector	Variable	Coefficient	Std. error	t-statistic	Prob.	R^2	Adjusted R^2
FMCG	C	0.0008	0.0004	2.0304	0.0425	0	0
CD	C	0.0003	0.0006	0.4410	0.6593	0	0
HC	C	0.0006	0.0003	1.8310	0.0674	0	0
Auto	C	0.0007	0.0005	1.3245	0.1856	0	0
Power	C	−0.0005	0.0006	−0.8929	0.3721	0	0
IT	C	0.0004	0.0006	0.6840	0.4941	0	0
Metal	C	−0.0003	0.0008	−0.4300	0.6673	0	0
ONG	C	−0.0002	0.0006	−0.3043	0.7609	0	0
TecK	C	0.0000	0.0005	0.0662	0.9472	0	0
PSU	C	−0.0001	0.0005	−0.1737	0.8622	0	0
Bank	C	0.0002	0.0007	0.2537	0.7998	0	0
SENSEX	C	0.0001	0.0005	0.0983	0.9217	0	0
CG	C	0.0007	0.000468	1.436277	0.1511	0	0

Table 4.58 Trading rule in BSE in post-crisis period

Sector	Variable	Coefficient	Std. error	t-statistic	Prob.	R^2	Adjusted R^2
FMCG	C	0.0004	0.0006	0.6678	0.5044	0.0007	−0.0002
	BUY60(−1)	0.0007	0.0008	0.8807	0.3787		
CD	C	−0.0016	0.0008	−1.9006	0.0576	0.0100	0.0091
	BUY60(−1)	0.0040	0.0012	3.3259	0.0009		
HC	C	0.0001	0.0005	0.2785	0.7807	0.0010	0.0001
	BUY60(−1)	0.0008	0.0007	1.0672	0.2861		
Auto	C	−0.0011	0.0007	−1.4598	0.1446	0.0106	0.0097
	BUY60(−1)	0.0035	0.0010	3.4193	0.0007		
Power	C	−0.0023	0.0008	−2.7289	0.0065	0.0083	0.0074
	BUY60(−1)	0.0035	0.0012	3.0257	0.0025		
IT	C	−0.0003	0.0008	−0.3611	0.7181	0.0016	0.0007
	BUY60(−1)	0.0016	0.0012	1.3474	0.1781		
Metal	C	−0.0024	0.0011	−2.2707	0.0234	0.00670	0.0058
	BUY60(−1)	0.0041	0.0015	2.7185	0.0067		
ONG	C	−0.0013	0.0008	−1.5333	0.1255	0.0028	0.0018
	BUY60(−1)	0.0021	0.0012	1.7364	0.0828		
TecK	C	−0.0006	0.0008	−0.7882	0.4308	0.0010	0.0001
	BUY60(−1)	0.0011	0.0011	1.0526	0.2928		
PSU	C	−0.0018	0.0007	−2.6357	0.0085	0.0114	0.0105
	BUY60(−1)	0.0035	0.0010	3.5499	0.0004		
Bank	C	−0.0006	0.0010	−0.6239	0.5328	0.0017	0.0008
	BUY60(−1)	0.0019	0.0014	1.3533	0.1762		
SENSEX	C	−0.0010	0.0008	−1.3827	0.1670	0.0040	0.0031
	BUY60(−1)	0.0023	0.0011	2.1007	0.0359		
CG	C	−0.00164	0.000678	−2.4224	0.0155	0.0122	0.0045
	BUY60(−1)	0.004581	0.000955	4.798367	0.0000		

4.10 The Optimal Trading Rule in India: The Epilogue

The present study has been an exploration into the possible presence of momentum or speculative trading in Indian stock market. The momentum trading, as mentioned earlier generates speculative bubble that might lead to panic and a financial market crash. This study is an attempt to look for the presence of persistent trends that could be fruitfully used by the investors along different stages of an economy. Specifically, it inquires whether EMH could be put on trial during a financial crisis and whether it is the human psychology, in the form of speculation and irrational exuberance, which drives or rather destabilizes a financial market.

The Indian stock market has been characterized by some significant latent structures. The structure, however, differs across the stock exchanges chosen. The Bombay Stock Exchange is characterized by a single structure where sectors and market are closely connected. The trend in the post-crisis period is, however, weaker than the 'average' (the trend for the entire period) market trend as well as the trend in the pre-crisis period. The BSE is always characterized by significant volatility with volatility clustering and asymmetric response of volatility toward good and bad news where volatility responds more toward bad news. The leverage effect is less pronounced in the post-crisis period compared to that in the entire period and in the pre-crisis period. The returns start falling and risks start mounting as the market plunges into a crisis. BSE is mostly characterized by a positive risk-return relationship. However, the correlation coefficient between risk and return starts declining and becomes negative as the market dips into crisis. The NSE is characterized by the presence of two latent structures, where the closely associated group of sectoral indexes dominates the market and is completely decoupled from the market index. Otherwise, the trends are quite similar to those obtained for BSE. Apart from the similarities in volatility trends and return cycles another trend is easily perceptible in the Indian stock market irrespective of the choice of the exchange. When the market experiences or passes through some 'extra-ordinary' events, some 'unique' or 'special' trend persists in the market. As the economy reverts back to its 'normal' state this 'special' trend weakens in the sense that the variability captured by the first factor declines steadily. For investors, this information might be extremely useful in designing profitable trading strategy. To be more specific, if it is possible to identify when this special trend would set in or how long it would last, investors might be able to design strategies to make profit out of market movements. The movements in the first factor Eigen value reveal few more observations. The Eigen value increases during the periods of recovery and reaches maximum just before the peak. During a stable period, however, the Eigen value falls or reaches a plateau. Therefore, the 'special' trend persists during the phases of recovery and weakens during the periods of recession or stability. The market crash could be predicted from a high Eigen value of the first factor and high Eigen value could be associated with market crash. In Indian context, hence, there is immense scope for the investors to use this piece of information to design profitable trading strategy in Bombay as well as the National Stock Exchange.

4.10 The Optimal Trading Rule in India: The Epilogue

As suggested by the portfolio construction rule, the risk-averse as well as risk-lover investors could find profitable investment opportunities in the Indian stock market. The choice of investment, however, has been much limited in the post-crisis period. This is particularly because of the low and even negative returns earned by many sectors in the post-crisis period. Significant trends persist so far as the nature of the sectors are concerned. While Metal and Consumer Goods sector avoided the crisis as members of BSE, they have been hard hit by the crisis in NSE. Pharmaceutical sector has emerged as profitable places of investment in the entire market as a whole after the crisis. FMCG and MNC are now offering profitable investment opportunity in NSE. FMCG, however, has lost profitability in BSE after crisis. Public Sector Units, Banks, Energy, Oil and Gas, Services, and the market indexes have been worst-hit by the crisis. The crisis, however, has transformed the defensive IT and the Financial Sector most aggressive.

Thus, the investors have immense scope in Indian market to design profitable investment strategies. The crisis, however, had significant impact on the possible portfolio construction. Definite trends exist in the market depending on the nature of the cycle of economy that could be profitably reaped by the investors. While the presence of such trends and opportunities raises doubt about the validity of the EMH in Indian context, the doubt might turn into belief if one looks at the long-term holding pattern in the market.

The Indian market is characterized by the presence of a long-term holding pattern. Almost all the indexes, irrespective of the choice of Exchanges, exhibit a profitable trading rule based on a 60 day moving average and IT shows a profitable trading rule at 30 day moving average. The trading pattern remains unaffected even after the crisis. The Indian market is thus not very myopic. Rather, it is quite pessimistic and risk averse.

Thus, Indian market, in the face of a global melt-down has been far from efficient. Definite trends and structures exist in the market that could be fruitfully used by the investors. Moreover, the market is characterized by presence of speculative trading and the crisis, in some cases had definite impacts on some aspects of the market rendering the EMH useless. The analysis of momentum trading, however, deserves special attention. The persistent presence of a sufficiently long holding period that is independent of the cycles of the economy reveals an important fact about the Indian stock market. The market is vulnerable on many counts: the EMH is on trial, the market is not "fundamentally stable", and the market trends are strong enough to attract momentum traders in the market. There is, however, one comfortable tone: it is perhaps not the human psychology that drives the Indian financial market. At least, it has been not so for the last financial melt-down of 2007–2008.

References

Basu S (1977) Investment performance of common stocks in relation to their price-earnings ratio: a test of the efficient market hypothesis. J Finan 32(3):663–682

Conrad J, Kaul G (1998) An anatomy of trading strategies. Rev Fin Stud 11:489–519

DeBondt WFM, Thaler RH (1985) Does the stock market overreact? J Finan 40:793–805

Fama E (1970) Efficient capital markets: a review of theory and empirical work. J Finan 25(2):383–417

Fama EF, French KR (1988) Permanent and temporary components of stock prices. J Polit Econ 96:246–273

Hawawini G, Keim DB (1995) On the predictability of common stock returns: world-wide evidence. Handbooks Oper Res Manage Sci 9:497–544

Jegadeesh N (1990) Evidence of predictable behaviour of security returns. J Finan 45:881–898

Jegadeesh N, Titman S (1993) Returns to buying winners and selling losers: implications for stock market efficiency. J Finan 48:65–91

Jegadeesh N, Titman S (1995) Overreaction, delayed reaction and contrarian profits. Rev Fin Stud 8:973–993

Lakonishok J, Smidt S (1988) Are seasonal anomalies real? A ninety-year perspective. Rev Fin Stud 1(4):403–425

Lee CMC, Bhaskaran S (2000) Price momentum and trading volume. J Finan 55:2017–2069

Liu W, Norman S, Xu X (1999) UK momentum tests. J Bus Finan Account 26(9/10):1043–1091

Lo AW, MacKinlay CA (1988) Stock prices do not follow random walks: evidence from a simple specification test. Rev Fin Stud 1(1):41–66

Mills TC, Coutts JA (1995) Calendar effects in the London stock exchange FT-SE indexes. Eur J Finan 1(1):79–94

Richards AJ (1997) Winner-Loser reversals in National stock market indices: Can they be explained? J Finan 52:2129–2144

Rouwenhorst KG (1998) International momentum strategies. J Finan 53:267–284

CPSIA information can be obtained at www.ICGtesting.com
Printed in the USA
LVOW100338300313

326808LV00004B/132/P